MESSAGE OF BIBLICAL SPIRITUALITY
Editorial Director: Carolyn Osiek, RSCJ

Volume 12

The Spirituality
of
Paul

Thomas H. Tobin, SJ

Michael Glazier
Wilmington, Delaware

About the Author

Thomas H. Tobin, SJ, is Associate Professor of Theology and Director of Graduate Studies in the Theology Department of Loyola University of Chicago. Among his other published books are *The Creation of Man: Philo and the History of Interpretation* and *Timaeus of Locri, On the Nature of the World and the Soul.*

The publisher wishes to acknowledge and thank *The Bible Today* for permission to use the map on page 18, copyright 1985 by The Order of St. Benedict, Inc.; published by The Liturgical Press, Collegeville, MN.

First published in 1987 by Michael Glazier, Inc., 1935 West Fourth Street, Wilmington, Delaware, 19805. ©1987 by Michael Glazier, Inc. All rights reserved. Library of Congress Catalog Card Number: 86-46354. International Standard Book Numbers: *Message of Biblical Spirituality* series: 0-89453-550-1, cloth; 0-89453-566-8, paper. THE SPIRITUALITY OF PAUL: 0-89453-562-5, cloth; 0-89453-578-1, paper. Typography by S. Almeida, Connie Runkel. Cover design by Florence Bern. Printed in the United States of America.

TABLE OF CONTENTS

5

ETHICAL PERSPECTIVES: THE SPIRIT AND SIN   98

6

ETHICS IN PRACTICE: FREEDOM AND COMMUNITY   118

7

SUFFERING AND HOPE FOR THE FUTURE   141

8

PAUL AND THE PEOPLE OF THE COVENANT   161

EDITOR'S PREFACE

One of the characteristics of church life today is a revived interest in spirituality. There is a growing list of resources in this area, yet the need for more is not exhausted. People are yearning for guidance in living an integrated life of faith in which belief, attitude, affections, prayer, and action form a cohesive unity which gives meaning to their lives.

The biblical tradition is a rich resource for the variety of ways in which people have heard God's call to live a life of faith and fidelity. In each of the biblical books we have a witness to the initiative of God in human history and to the attempts of people not so different from ourselves to respond to the revelation of God's love and care.

The fifteen volumes in the *Message of Biblical Spirituality* series aim to provide ready access to the treasury of biblical faith. Modern social science has made us aware of how the particular way in which one views reality conditions the ways in which one will interpret experience and life itself. Each volume in this series is an attempt to retell and interpret the biblical story from within the faith perspective that originally formed it. Each seeks to portray what it is like to see God, the world, and oneself from a particular point of view and to search for ways to respond faithfully to that vision. We who are citizens of our twentieth century world cannot be people of the ancient biblical world, but we can grow closer to their experience and their faith and thus closer to God, through the living Word of God which is the Bible.

The series includes an international group of authors representing England, Ireland, Canada, and the United States, but whose life experience has included first-hand knowledge of many other countries. All are proven scholars and committed believers whose faith is as important to them as their scholarship. Each acts as interpreter of one part of the biblical tradition in order to enable its spiritual vitality to be passed on to others. It is our hope that through their labor the reader will be able to enter more deeply into the life of faith, hope, and love through a fuller understanding of and appreciation for the biblical Word as handed down to us by God's faithful witnesses, the biblical authors themselves.

Carolyn Osiek, RSCJ
Associate Professor of New Testament Studies
Catholic Theological Union, Chicago

INTRODUCTION

Spirituality is an often used and sometimes abused word. Some use the term to mean the way in which the outlooks and beliefs of a particular religious tradition are appropriated and practiced in everyday life. Others mean by the term a kind of spiritual path which leads to enlightenment. Still others use it to refer to the ascetical practices of a religious tradition. Again, still others think of it as the religious sensibility engendered by a particular religious tradition. Many of these definitions overlap, but each reflects a somewhat different understanding of the term spirituality.

In this book I shall use the term rather broadly, to refer especially to the religious sensibilities of Paul. By religious sensibilities I mean the result of the interaction between Paul's own experience of God and of Christ and the Christian tradition to which he came to be committed. The two (Paul's own experience and Christian tradition) obviously are not separate, but they can be distinguished in the sense that Paul's own experience not only was influenced and formed by Christian tradition but also colored and transformed that tradition as he appropriated it in living out his life as a Christian. This interaction affects Paul's view of himself, of God and Christ, and of his relationships to the Christian communities that he either founded or of which he was a part.

In Christianity the term spirituality has sometimes been used to distinguish dogmatic or systematic theology, which deals with the doctrines of the Christian faith, from spiritual theology or spirituality which deals with the way in which that faith is to be lived out in everyday life. In this context the two have often been set off against one another. Some see systematic theology as a rather dry, rigid, "dogmatic," even lifeless set of doctrines, and spirituality as the life-giving practice at the center of Christian tradition. On the other hand, some see spirituality as a sincere but rather muddle-headed attempt to simplify the complexities and depths of the Christian tradition. In either case, the two rest uneasily side by side.

This tension between "theology" and "spirituality" has, of course, been destructive to both. It has led to precisely the unhealthy consequences pointed out by both camps. Theology comes to seem irrelevant, and spirituality comes to seem lacking in depth or substance. The love of God and the desire for learning are no longer two inseparable aspects of one reality.

Fortunately many Christians are coming to see that such a dichotomy should not and need not continue to exist. A deep and at the same time rigorous understanding of the Christian faith can contribute to the way in which Christians live their lives; and a sensitivity to the religious sensibilities of the Christian tradition can serve to deepen not only faith but one's understanding of that faith, that is, theology.

Perhaps the most important and also the easiest area where these two elements can come together is in the interpretation of the Bible. It is the most important area because Christians understand the Bible as, in some sense, the inspired word of God. It is the easiest because the Bible itself is not a theological treatise. It is a complex of different kinds of writings, narratives, poetry, proverbs, letters, and apocalypses, to name but a few. In order to understand that complex body of literature, one must be sensitive to all of the various ways in which human beings have expressed themselves in writing over the centuries. The Bible does not allow for only one kind of interpretation.

When one tries to understand the religious sensibilities of a biblical writer, in this case Paul, one needs to be aware of another pitfall of interpretation. Because the Bible is regarded by Christians as inspired, one is tempted to look on what one finds in a biblical text, again, for example, the letters of Paul, as normative in a rather narrow sense. One is tempted simply to take the perspectives of Paul as the perspectives that one must have as a Christian. Such a viewpoint takes no account of the historical character of the biblical writings. These texts came from particular times and particular places and were intended for audiences in particular situations. There may be similarities between their times, places, and situations and ours, but they are not the same. To treat them as the same is in a real sense to be unfaithful to the biblical texts themselves. The Bible is not timeless but timely. The various books of the Bible were written to be relevant to particular times and situations. If they had not been significant in their own situations, they never would have been preserved.

Yet, when one reads the Bible as a Christian, what one reads is not simply texts of merely historical interest. The Biblical writings are not simply descriptions of what some far-away people from a time long past thought about God and their own destinies. Rather, Christians understand these writings as still relevant for them, as still having a claim on them, as still throwing light on their own lives. They are of much more than antiquarian interest.

In interpreting the Bible, then, one must try to be true to both the meaning of a biblical text in its own historical context and the value that the text has or can have for later generations of Christians. When one reads the Bible as a Christian, the first, if not the fundamental, act of faith is one in which one trusts that by putting one's own experience and that of one's own world next to the experience and world of the Biblical text, light will be shed on both. It is to trust that the dialogue between the reader and the biblical text will bring to light similarities or analogies between our experience and theirs in such a way that we will better understand not only the text but also our own experience, our world, and our relationship to God. If one reads the Bible in this sort of way, then one can be true both to the complexities of the biblical text and to the legitimate claims of one's own experience and the challenges of one's own world.

Paul is one of the easiest and most fascinating biblical authors with which to do this. It is comparatively easy to talk about the spirituality of Paul. Part of the reason for this is the simple fact that Paul wrote letters. What we have preserved from Paul himself are the letters which he wrote to various Christian communities in Asia Minor, Greece, and Rome. In those letters he dealt with how to live out one's life as a Christian and the problems that these various Christian communities were having in living out their commitment. Our access to the real life of these communities is rather direct; Paul writes directly to them about their problems and their accomplishments. This is in contrast to what can be learned from a reading of the gospels. In each of the gospels we read the various narratives and sayings connected with the life, death, and resurrection of Jesus. But we do not learn directly about either the religious sensibilities of the gospel writers or about the communities out of which the gospels came or to which they were directed. Rather we are forced to analyze the ways in which each of the gospel writers tells the story of Jesus' words and deeds and then infer the basic outlook which that gospel writer had about Jesus and how that outlook reflected both his own religious sensibilities and those of his community. When one reads Paul's letters, however, one deals directly with both Paul's religious outlooks and concerns and the religious outlooks and concerns of the communities to which he wrote.

In addition, one comes to know the man himself through his letters in a way that is impossible when one tries to come to know the authors of the four gospels. One gets a chance to see how Paul practices what he preaches. One also gets a chance to see how Paul lives up to the demands which he makes of the communities with which he deals. While Paul's letters (or what can be learned from the Acts of the Apostles) do not allow us to reconstruct a full life of Paul, they do allow us to get to know the man and what moves him in a way that is impossible for any other New Testament author.

This portrait of Paul will not always be flattering but it will have a three-dimensional character which we can have with no other New Testament writer. One of the most interesting and rewarding aspects of reading Paul's letters is that one comes in close contact with a first-century Christian who is struggling along with other early Christians to make sense of experiences which have transformed both his and their lives.

As I mentioned above, the portrait that emerges from reading Paul's letters is a three-dimensional one. It is also a very human one. Paul was a man of immense energy, immense drive, immense commitment to what he was doing. But he was also a man whose patience often wore thin and whose temper was short. He could be deeply generous and kind; yet at the same time he had a genius for invective. He could at once praise the centrality of Christian freedom and demand that one of his communities handle a problem his way. He believed deeply in the movement of the Holy Spirit in the Christian community, but he also believed in the correctness of his own central insights into the Christian message, no matter what other Christians did or did not believe. Paul is both exasperating and exhilarating. One is likely to love Paul or to hate him, or to love him and hate him at the same time. Few people remain indifferent toward him. Both his virtues and his vices have contributed to his fascination to men and women down through the ages.

I shall begin by looking at the life of Paul (Chapter One). Although one can hardly write a biography of Paul, more is known of his life than that of any other New Testament writer. What we do know of his life as it emerges from his letters and to a certain extent from the Acts of the Apostles gives us a sense of what drove Paul and, even more importantly, what changed Paul.

The next two chapters (Chapters Two and Three) will examine Paul's experience on the road to Damascus and, more generally, his understanding of God and Christ. These two chapters form a unity in the sense that Paul's view of God and of Christ were deeply colored by his "call" or "conversion" experience on the road to Damascus.

The fourth chapter will deal with Paul's understanding of the relationship of faith in Christ to the Mosaic Law. Paul always saw himself as a believing Jew, as someone who believed deeply in the promises made to Abraham and to Moses. He was therefore compelled to try to understand what was the effect of his faith in Christ, and the salvation of the Gentiles through that faith, on the status of the Mosaic Law.

The next two chapters (Chapters Five and Six) are concerned with the way in which faith in Christ was to be lived out in everyday life. Here we will deal with both the overall ethical perspectives that dominate Paul's thought and with several specific ethical issues that were of importance to Paul. In this way one can get a sense of both general outlook and concrete application.

Finally, the last two chapters (Chapters Seven and Eight) will deal with the closely related issues of human suffering and Christian eschatology (Christian hope about the consummation of the world). Here we will deal with how Paul attempts to reconcile the fact of human suffering with his faith in a gracious God. We shall also deal with what was for Paul the most difficult and mysterious of all problems, the fact that, for the most part, his fellow Jews had not come to have faith in Christ. His anguished reflections on this issue forced him to bring together all of his deepest convictions about the mysterious providence of a gracious God and his hopes for universal salvation.

As we look at each of these issues, I shall try to let Paul

speak for himself. He is a master rhetorician and so his thought is inextricably tied up with the words that he uses. I shall try as best as I can to interpret those words, to set them in context, to see the patterns into which they fall. But in the end one must always return to the words of Paul himself in all of their density and power.

Perhaps the most characteristic feature of Paul's spirituality is his willingness to hold in tension the contrasting elements in his life. As we shall see, Paul's own religious experience plays a decisive role in the decisions that he makes. Yet he is equally convinced that his experience must in some fashion be reconciled with what he has been given in both Jewish and Christian tradition. For Paul such a reconciliation can never be simply splitting the difference; rather it must be a resolution in which he is true to both poles of the tension. This same is true for other polarities in Paul's religious sensibilities: power and weakness, freedom and community, Jew and Gentile, present and future. In each case Paul tries to do justice to both poles of the tension.

Because of these polarities, Paul's religious thought is both complex and often elusive. It is not the work of a systematician but of someone who tries to live out his basic convictions in the particular situations in which he finds himself. While there is a consistency in the basic convictions and polarities out of which he lives, the arguments that he uses to support those convictions or reconcile those polarities depend a great deal on the concrete situation with which he finds himself dealing. Thus, while there are patterns to Paul's thought, those patterns are not altogether predictable nor can they be reduced to a completely consistent system.

In the end, this unpredictability contributes to our fascination with Paul. One comes to know someone who is struggling with the basic issues of human existence and who is trying to understand them as best as he can. He is trying to make sense of the messiness of life rather than create the tidiness of a completely consistent system.

In order to allow the reader to become familiar with Paul in a translation that is easily accessible for future study, biblical quotations used throughout are from the Revised Standard Version.

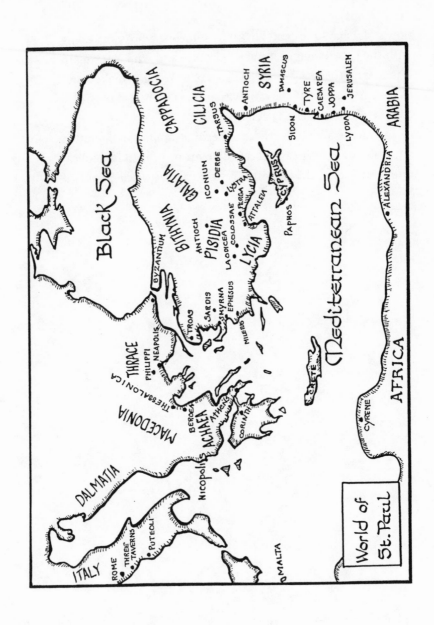

1

THE LIFE OF PAUL

We know more about the life of Paul than we do about any other New Testament author. Much of what we know of Paul's life comes from information we can gather from his letters to various early Christian communities that he founded. Other information about his life comes from the Acts of the Apostles, the second half of which focuses on Paul's career.

Yet much of this information has to be used with caution. Much of what is found in Paul's letters reflects the controversies in which Paul was involved, and so it has to be used with the same caution that one would use in evaluating any work of a polemical character. The information about Paul's life found in the Acts of the Apostles comes from a generation after Paul's death and reflects its author's attempt to integrate Paul into the author's own view of the history of early Christianity. It too, then, must be used with caution.

Granted all of those cautions, we still know more of Paul's life than we do of any other New Testament author. This knowledge, limited though it may be, allows us to set Paul's letters in the context of his life in a way that is impossible for the works of other New Testament authors. This is especially important in the case of Paul because the religious convictions found in his letters are so deeply imbedded in his own religious experience and missionary career.

The Early Life of Paul

According to the Acts of the Apostles (9:11; 21:39; 22:3) Paul was born in Tarsus in Cilicia, a prominent trading center in the southeastern corner of Asia Minor (present-day Turkey). The date of his birth is not certain, but it probably was around A.D. 10. From Philippians 3:5 we learn that he was a Jew of the tribe of Benjamin and was circumcised on the eighth day. He also tells us in that same verse that he was a Pharisee by conviction. He probably had both a Roman name (Paul) and a Jewish name (Saul) (Acts 7:58; 8:1).

From the way in which his letters were written, Paul clearly had both a good Jewish education and a good Greek education. His letters reflect a deep knowledge of the Hebrew Scriptures and their interpretation as well as a detailed acquaintance with Greek rhetoric. While his knowledge of Greek rhetoric was certainly obtained at Tarsus, it is more difficult to imagine that he obtained his knowledge of the interpretation of the Hebrew Scriptures at Tarsus, especially since that knowledge seems to have involved a formal Pharisaic education. The Pharisees were a Palestinian sect within Judaism. While there may have been Pharisaic Jews outside of Palestine, the kind of formal Pharisaic education reflected in Paul's letters was possible only in Palestine itself. Acts 22:3

claims that Paul studied at the feet of Rabbi Gamaliel I in Jerusalem. Gamaliel I was a prominent Palestinian rabbi of the first century. While it is difficult to evaluate the trustworthiness of that particular claim, it does seem likely that some time before his call or conversion to belief in Christ Paul came to Jerusalem and studied the Pharisaic interpretation of the Scriptures.

Acts 22:25-29 also claims that Paul had inherited Roman citizenship from his father. Paul, however, makes no such claim for himself. In fact, this seems unlikely since, as a Roman citizen, he would have been exempt from the punishments that he claims to have received in 2 Corinthians 11:24-25.

The two most prominent aspects of his life prior to his belief in Christ were his observance of the law as a Pharisee and his persecution of those who believed in Christ (Phil 3:5-6; Gal 1:13, 23; 1 Cor 15:9). He describes his observance of the Mosaic Law as "blameless" (Phil 3:6). While granting a certain amount of exaggeration on Paul's part, he certainly saw himself as a committed, observant Jew. It was out of this commitment to Judaism that Paul became involved in the persecution of those who believed in Christ.

It is not altogether clear what this persecution actually involved or what the real motivation behind it was. One has to remember that, at this early stage of Christianity, Christians saw themselves as members of the Jewish community, Jews who believed in Jesus as the Messiah. They saw themselves not as members of a new religion, but as a sect well within the borders of Judaism. The accounts of his persecution of believers in Christ in Acts (8:3; 9:1; 26:9-12) have to be viewed with a great deal of caution. In Acts Paul is described as first persecuting Christians in Jerusalem. He arrests them and throws them into prison and then, when they are faced with a sentence of death, he votes against them (Acts 26:10). In addition, he tries to persecute them even in foreign cities (Acts 26:11). Armed with letters from the high priest to the synagogues in Damascus, he sets out for Damascus in order to bring any believers in Christ back to Jerusalem for punishment (Acts 9:1).

There are, however, significant problems with the veracity of this account in the Acts of the Apostles. In the first place, it seems that neither the high priest nor the Sanhedrin had the authority to impose the death sentence on their own. Such a sentence could be imposed only with the approval of the Roman authorities. Secondly, it is very unlikely that either the high priest or the Sanhedrin had any authority to take believers in Christ from beyond the borders of Palestine and bring them back to Jerusalem for punishment. A more likely explanation for the persecution is that Paul was involved in subjecting Christians to the normal punishments of the synagogue which involved exclusion from the Jewish community, an exclusion which may have had other social or economic consequences. It did not, however, involve either capital punishment or imprisonment.

One can also only speculate on Paul's reasons for persecuting those who believed in Jesus. During this time period, other Jews made messianic claims, but their followers seem not to have been persecuted as were the followers of Jesus. This has led some scholars to suggest that the real motivation for Paul's persecution may have been some early Christians' attitude toward the observance of the Mosaic Law, an observance about which Paul himself had deep convictions. Some early Christians may have had an attitude toward the observance of the Mosaic Law that Paul and other Jews like him found intolerably lax. He may have felt that such an attitude endangered the very foundations of Judaism as he understood it. In this view, it was not these early Christians' belief in Jesus as the Messiah but their attitude toward the Mosaic Law that enraged Paul.

Yet one suspects that it was a combination of both their belief in Jesus and their attitude toward the Law which angered Paul. Early Christians undoubtedly appealed to the figure of Jesus and his words in order to justify their attitude toward the observance or non-observance of the Mosaic Law. Because their attitude toward the Law was rooted in their belief in Jesus, Paul, therefore, would have found both elements of Christian belief objectionable.

Call, First Missionary Journey, and the Council in Jerusalem

It was on a journey to Damascus to continue his "persecution" of Christians that Paul experienced something that would change his life forever. That experience was of the risen Jesus whom God the Father had revealed to him (Gal 1:15-16). As Paul understood that experience, it was not simply a revelation of Jesus; it was also a call to preach Jesus to the Gentiles. A conclusion that Paul drew from his experience of the risen Jesus and his call to preach to the Gentiles was that the Mosaic Law had come to an end. We shall go into more detail about that central experience in Paul's life in the next chapter. For the moment what is important to keep in mind is that Paul saw both his preaching to the Gentiles and the end of the Mosaic Law as central elements of his experience of the risen Jesus.

This experience took place about A.D. 35. For the next three years, Paul's missionary work on behalf of Christianity centered around the city of Damascus and the area to the south and east of that city (Gal 1:17). Paul himself says that he did not go up to Jerusalem to meet with the Church's leaders there until three years later, that is in A.D. 38 (Gal 1:18). At that time he went to Jerusalem and met with Peter and with James (Gal 1:19-20). Paul does not tell us what took place during that meeting or what issues were discussed. The visit to Jerusalem mentioned in Acts 9:26-30 probably refers to this visit.

Paul began his missionary activities in areas that were largely Gentile. This is important because it means that Paul's first experiences of being a believer in the risen Jesus were worked out in an environment that was quite different from the Jewish-Christian environment of the Jerusalem Church. It was undoubtedly as a part of this environment and as a member of Christian communities in this environment that Paul developed his own understanding of what was central to belief in Jesus.

After his return from his first visit to Jerusalem, Paul worked for the next ten years (A.D. 38-48) in the regions of Syria and Cilicia (Gal 1:21). His travels during this period make up his first missionary journey. During this time the base of his activities was probably Antioch in Syria (Acts 11:25-26). Outside of Jerusalem itself, Antioch was probably the main center of early Christianity at this time. The make-up of the Christian community at Antioch differed signifi-cantly from that of Jerusalem. The Antiochene community was probably made up largely of Gentile Christian converts. While this community shared with the Christians of Jerusalem their beliefs in Jesus, they probably did not share the Jerusalem community's belief in the continuing validity of the Mosaic Law. Made up largely of Gentile Christians this community did not continue to observe the Mosaic Law.

Over the period of the ten years that Paul used Antioch as a base of his operations, the tension between the Christians of Antioch and those of Jerusalem over the question of the continuing validity of the Mosaic Law built up. This tension may have been brought to a head when Jewish Christians from Jerusalem came to Antioch and claimed that all Christians, whether Jewish or Gentile, had to be circumcised and observe the Mosaic Law in order to be true Christians (Acts 15:1). Paul and other Antiochene Christians objected to this position.

In order to clear up this difficulty, Paul as part of a delegation of Christians from Antioch went up to Jerusalem to meet with the leaders of the Jerusalem Church. This meeting took place in A.D. 48. It is described both in Galatians 2:1-10 and in Acts 15:1-35. Even granted the polemical tone of Paul's account of the meeting, Galatians 2:1-10 is probably the more reliable of the two accounts. In that account of the meeting Paul claims that the two sides came to an agreement. The "pillars of the Church" in Jerusalem, James, Peter, and John, agreed that the Gospel that Paul and others were preaching to the Gentiles, a Gospel without circumcision and observance of the Mosaic Law, was legitimate. On the other hand, Paul and the rest of the delegation from Antioch agreed that the Gospel preached by the Jewish Christians of Jerusalem to their fellow Jews, a Gospel which included circumcision and observance of the Mosaic Law, was also legitimate. Paul describes this compromise in Galatians 2:6-9:

> 6And from those who were reputed to be something (what they were makes no difference to me: God shows no partiality)— those, I say, who were of repute added nothing to me; 7but on the contrary, when they saw that I had been entrusted with the gospel to the uncircumcised, just as Peter had been entrusted with the gospel to the circumcised 8(for he who worked through Peter for the mission to the circumcised worked through me also for the Gentiles), 9and when they perceived the grace that was given to me, James and Cephas and John, who were reputed to be pillars, gave to me and Barnabas the right hand of fellowship, that we should go to the Gentiles and they to the circumcision.

In return for their acceptance, Paul and the other members of the delegation agreed to remember the "poor" of the Jerusalem Church. As becomes clear from Paul's letters (e.g., 2 Cor 8–9), this meant a collection among the Gentile Christian Churches for the poor of the Jerusalem Church.

What does not emerge from Paul's account of this meeting in Jerusalem was the inherent instability of this compromise, an instability that would plague Paul for much of his career. At a practical level, the compromise could work only if Gentile Christians and Jewish Christians were never together in the same community. If they were together, whose position on the observance of the Mosaic Law would prevail? For example, if they ate together, would the dietary regulations of the Mosaic Law be observed or not?

At a deeper level, the logic of the two positions were irreconcilable. Paul's position, as we shall see in more detail in a later chapter, was that observance of the Mosaic Law was no longer necessary for either Gentile Christians or Jewish Christians. In the same way, if, as many Jewish Christians believed, the Mosaic Law was still in force, then its observance should be required of both Jewish Christians and Gentile Christians. The compromise, then, was inherently unstable and, in the course of Paul's later missionary journeys, would break apart and cause Paul a great deal of trouble.

In fact, the compromise began to unravel almost immediately. After the end of the conference, Paul and his delegation returned to Antioch. Soon after that, probably in the fall of A.D. 48, Peter came to Antioch. When he first arrived, Peter took part in the common meals with the Gentile Christians. Soon after that, however, supporters of James came to Antioch from Jerusalem. At this point Peter withdrew from eating the common meals with Gentile Christians. This was due to the concern of James' supporters over keeping the various Jewish dietary laws. Other Jewish Christians, including Barnabas, followed Peter's example. Paul challenged Peter over what he considered Peter's hypocrisy. He angrily demanded of Peter how he (Peter), though a Jew, could live like a Gentile and then turn around and act in such a way that compelled Gentiles to live like Jews (Gal 2:12). His point was that, since Peter was willing to forego observance of the dietary laws when he first came to Antioch, his later withdrawal from table fellowship because of pressure from James' supporters was hypocritical.

Second Missionary Journey

Soon after this confrontation with Peter, Paul left Antioch on his second missionary journey (A.D. 49-52). Because Paul did not mention in the narration of his confrontation with Peter (Gal 2:11-14) that his own view of the matter prevailed, Paul may have lost this battle, and that loss may have been the principal reason why he left Antioch. Paul's traveling companions on this journey were Silvanus (Silas) and, a bit later in the journey, Timothy.

Paul first traveled through Syria and Cilicia, stopping at towns that he had visited earlier. He then moved north through Galatia and then west through western Asia Minor to Troas. He stayed several months in the region of Galatia and founded several communities there. Acts 16:9-10 describes a vision that Paul had at Troas in which he saw a Macedonian standing and beseeching him to come to Macedonia.

As a result of this vision Paul crossed over into Greece. He landed at the city of Neapolis and then travelled inland a few miles to Philippi. After founding a community at Philippi, he was forced to leave the city because of some sort of persecution (1 Thess 2:2). He then moved on to Thessalonica, the most important city of Macedonia. From there Paul traveled on to Athens. While Paul's speech on the Areopagus in Acts 17:22-31 is clearly a Lukan composition, he may have founded a community in Athens during his stay there.

In late A.D. 50, he arrived in Corinth and probably stayed there until the spring of A.D. 52. He used Corinth as the base of his operations for the next year and a half. While he arrived at Corinth with only Silvanus and Timothy, he soon gathered around him other Christians who participated in his missionary work. Paul stayed with Priscilla and Aquila, two wealthy Jewish Christians who had come to Corinth after being expelled from Rome by an edict of the Roman emperor Claudius. He was also joined by Stephanas (1 Cor 16:15) and

Apollos, a Jewish Christian from Alexandria (Acts 18:24).

Paul's lengthy stay in Corinth and the presence of a number of co-workers are important correctives to an overly romantic notion of Paul's missionary journeys. First, he was not traveling all of the time. Rather he seems to have settled in one place, first Corinth and later Ephesus. Second, Paul was not simply a lonely missionary traveling around the eastern Mediterranean basin. Rather, he was beginning to develop a larger, more organized missionary effort which involved a number of other people in his work.

One of the ways in which he kept up contact with communities that he had founded was through the use of letters. The first of the letters which have been preserved for us comes from this period. It is 1 Thessalonians and was probably written to the Thessalonian Christian community from Corinth in the winter of A.D. 51. The letter is made up primarily of encouragement and advice for the new Christian community at Thessalonica (1 Thess 1–3).

The last section of the letter (1 Thess 4:13–5:11) is concerned with the second coming of Christ (the *parousia*). Early Christians, Paul included, expected that Christ's coming in glory would be soon. Yet the Thessalonian Christians were troubled by the fact that several of their members had already died. They wondered what their fate would be at the coming of Christ in glory. This problem may have been the immediate reason why Paul wrote the letter. Paul consoled the Thessalonian Christians with his conviction that at Christ's coming those Christians who had died would be raised and would go to meet the Lord along with those Christians who were still alive. Those who had died would be at no disadvantage. In addition, Paul emphasized to them that Christ's coming would be unexpected and so they should always be prepared for it by the quality of their present lives.

Paul's stay in Corinth came to an end in the spring of A.D. 52. The reason why Paul left Corinth is not clear. According to Acts 18:12-28, he was brought before the Roman proconsul Gallio by Jews in Corinth who claimed that he was trying to persuade people to worship God contrary to the Law (Acts 18:12-13). According to Acts, Gallio dismissed the suit, claiming that the dispute between Paul and the Jews was a matter of Jewish Law and not of concern to him (Acts 18:14-15).

Since the author of Acts is at pains to put the Roman proconsul in a favorable light, many of the details of the story may be legendary. Yet it may reflect a dispute between Paul and his largely Gentile Christian community on the one side and observant Jews on the other. The fact that the largely Gentile Christian community of Corinth was claiming to be part of the Jewish tradition and yet did not observe the Mosaic Law would have been clearly objectionable to observant Jews. The story in Acts 18:12-18 may reflect that dispute, and the dispute may have been one of the causes for Paul's leaving Corinth.

Third Missionary Journey

After leaving Corinth in the spring of A.D. 52, Acts 18:18-23 tells us that Paul returned to Antioch in Syria by way of Ephesus. Acts 18:22 seems to indicate that he also made a trip to Jerusalem. The details of this journey are very sparse and difficult to evaluate historically. In any case, he seems to have ended up in Ephesus again by the end of A.D.

52, after passing through much of Asia Minor, including a brief visit to the Galatian Christians. This is Paul's third missionary journey. During this journey his center of activity was at Ephesus, a major city on the western coast of Asia Minor. He stayed there from the end of A.D. 52 until the spring of A.D. 55.

During his lengthy stay at Ephesus Paul wrote several of the letters which have been preserved for us. These letters (Galatians, Philippians, 1 Corinthians, and part of 2 Corinthians) reflect the various controversies in which Paul became involved as he kept up contact with the Christian communities that he had had a part in founding. Since we know of these controversies only through Paul's letters, we have only one side of the story. The positions taken by his opponents can be reconstructed only through Paul's often very polemical reaction to them. These reconstructions, then, are often hypothetical.

The first of these letters was probably to the Galatians, written early in Paul's stay at Ephesus (A.D. 52-53). Soon after Paul's second visit to the Galatian Christians (Gal 4:13) on his way to Ephesus, Jewish Christian missionaries, probably connected with Jerusalem, arrived in Galatia. They tried to persuade the Galatian Christians that Gentile converts not only had to believe in Christ but also that they had to be circumcised and observe the Mosaic Law, including its ritual prescriptions.

Paul was utterly opposed to this and wrote an angry letter to the Galatian Christians arguing that to be circumcised and obey the Mosaic Law was to compromise their belief in Christ (Gal 2:15-21). If they observed the Mosaic Law, they were tacitly admitting that belief in Christ was insufficient for salvation, that in fact Christ had died to no purpose. Paul then went on to offer a series of proofs (Gal 3:1—4:31), some of which were derived from his interpretations of Scripture, to emphasize his position.

A much more complicated controversy arose between Paul and the Christian community at Corinth. As best as we can reconstruct that controversy, it went through several stages and lasted from late A.D. 53 through the summer of A.D. 55. The catalyst for the first stage of the controversy seems to have been the appearance of factions within the Corinthian Christian community (1 Cor 1:10-17). Each of these factions within the community claimed that they had been initiated into a special, higher knowledge through the person who had baptized them. They were filled with a special wisdom. This special wisdom had so transformed them that they were now already leading the life of the resurrection. Death would simply be the sloughing off of the body (1 Cor 15:12-19). The ethical consequences of these beliefs varied wildly. One group of Corinthian Christians approved of a man who was living with his step-mother (1 Cor 5:1-8) while another group disapproved even of conventional marriages between Christians (1 Cor 7:1-7).

Paul countered their claims to a superior wisdom by emphasizing that the wisdom of God had made foolishness of human wisdom. The cross of Christ had turned human wisdom on its head. The wisdom of God was a real wisdom, but it was very unlike any form of human wisdom. Because of this the Corinthians' claim to possess a higher wisdom was really foolishness (1 Cor 1:18-2:16). Their foolishness, according to Paul, became most apparent when it created factions within the Corinthian community. Paul argued that these factions reflected the spiritual immaturity of the Corinthian Christians since they made a mockery of the fact that it was God who was supposed to be at work in the community through Christ. The Corinthian Christians were, in effect, dividing up Christ (1 Cor 3:1-17).

Paul also argued against the extreme ethical positions taken by the Corinthian Christians. He condemned the man who was living in incest (1 Cor 5:1-8) and affirmed the value of Christian marriage (1 Cor 7:1-16). We will look at these examples more carefully when we discuss Paul's view of ethics. But for the moment what is important to notice is Paul's emphasis on a responsible Christian freedom, a freedom that takes the sensibilities and limitations of one's fellow Christians into serious consideration.

Finally Paul argues that there is a tension in Christians' lives between the "already" of Christ's coming and the "not yet" of the final consummation of the world. The final resurrection is still in the future; it is not already present in such a way that Christians have nothing more to look forward to (1 Cor 15).

We do not know what the effect of this letter was on the situation in Corinth. But from 2 Corinthians we do know that the situation in Corinth quickly changed, but not for the better. 2 Corinthians seems to be a composite letter made up of fragments from several letters that Paul wrote to the Corinthian Christians during these controversies:

—2 Cor 2:14-6:13; 7:2-4: Letter of Defense (spring A.D. 54, from Ephesus)
—2 Cor 10–13: Letter Written in Tears (see 2 Cor 2:4; 7:8) (summer A.D. 54, from Ephesus)

—2 Cor 1:1–2:13; 7:5-16: Letter of Reconciliation (summer A.D. 55, from Macedonia)
—2 Cor 8 and 9: Letters of Recommendation (summer A.D. 55, from Macedonia)

Soon after Paul's first letter to the Corinthians, a group of Jewish Christian missionaries seem to have arrived at Corinth. This group seems to have appealed to some of the same elements in the Corinthian community against which Paul had written in 1 Corinthians. They emphasized that their preaching contained a higher kind of wisdom, certainly higher than that preached by Paul (see 2 Cor 10:5). But unlike the opponents of 1 Corinthians, this group of missionaries emphasized the Jewish aspects of their religious message. Unlike the Jewish Christian missionaries who preached to the Galatian Christians, however, these missionaries did not emphasize the observance of the Mosaic Law so much as the renewal of the Jewish religion through a spiritual interpretation of the Scriptures (2 Cor 3:4-18) and the working of powerful deeds and miracles (2 Cor 12:11-12). They represented a kind of viewpoint found more often in Hellenistic Judaism than in the Judaism of Palestine represented by the Jewish Christian missionaries who came to Galatia.

Their claims challenged not only the gospel that Paul had been preaching but also his identity as an apostle. They claimed that while Paul's letters may have been impressive, his physical presence and his speech were of no account (2 Cor 10:10). For the next year (spring of A.D. 54 through the spring of A.D 55) Paul carried on a running battle with the Corinthian Christians over the influence of these Hellenistic Jewish Christian missionaries. At first Paul wrote the Corinthian

Christians a letter (the Letter of Defense: 2 Cor 2:14–6:13; 7:2-4) defending both his interpretation of the Christian message (2 Cor 3:7-18) and his ministry of preaching that message (2 Cor 4:1–6:10). He defended his preaching of the Christian message by asserting that it came through the power of the Spirit (2 Cor 3:6, 8) and not through some esoteric interpretation of the Scriptures (2 Cor 3:6 ff). In addition he defended his own apostolate by saying that he preached Jesus Christ without the cunning and underhanded ways used by his opponents at Corinth (2 Cor 4:2, 5).

After writing the letter, he himself made a visit to Corinth, probably in the summer of A.D. 54, in order to clear up the situation (2 Cor 2:1; 12:21). This visit was not at all successful; it seems rather to have made the situation worse. Paul refers to this visit to Corinth as the "painful visit" (2 Cor 2:1), and he probably left Corinth in anger and returned to Ephesus.

After his return to Ephesus Paul wrote the Corinthians another letter (the Letter Written in Tears: 2 Cor 10-13) during the winter of A.D. 54-55. In this letter, one of the most rhetorical that he ever wrote, he heatedly defends his ministry against the contempt of his opponents. In 2 Corinthians 11:16–12:13 he lists all of his accomplishments as an apostle as a challenge to those who had belittled his work. Yet he sets himself apart from his opponents by emphasizing not his accomplishments but his weaknesses and claiming that it was through his weaknesses that God really was at work in his ministry (2 Cor 12:1-10).

We do not know what the effect of this letter was. But in addition to sending the letter, Paul also sent one of his co-workers, Titus, to the Corinthian Christians. Titus seems to have served as an intermediary between Paul and the

Corinthians. In the summer of A.D. 55 Paul left Ephesus and went to Macedonia in northern Greece. There he met Titus who brought him news of the reconciliation between Paul and the Corinthian community. From Macedonia Paul wrote another letter to the Corinthians (the Letter of Reconciliation: 2 Cor 1:1–2:13; 7:5-16) in the summer of A.D. 55. While Paul was still a bit defensive about his conduct during the controversy (2 Cor 1:12-14), he asked the Corinthian community to forgive and to be reconciled with those members of the community who had sided with his opponents (2 Cor 2:5-11).

The lengthy controversy with the Corinthian Christians was not the only difficulty that Paul experienced during his stay in Ephesus. During the winter of A.D. 54-55 Paul may have spent some time in prison. This imprisonment seems to be reflected in 2 Corinthians 1:8-11 and Philippians 1:12-26. We do not know the reason for that imprisonment, but it may have been connected with the riot of silversmiths described in Acts 19:21-41. According to Acts the Ephesian silversmiths rioted against the Christians because they thought that Christian rejection of pagan cults was damaging their business of selling silver shrines of Artemis, a Greek goddess who had a shrine at Ephesus.

It was probably during this imprisonment that Paul wrote his letters to the Philippians and to Philemon. The letter to Philemon is the only letter of Paul that was written to an individual. In it Paul asks Philemon, a Christian living at Colossae, to take back without punishment one of his runaway slaves, Onesimus (Phlm 4-22).

During this imprisonment Paul also carried on a correspondence with the Christians of Philippi in northern Greece. Like 2 Corinthians, our present letter to the Philippians seems to be a composite letter. Philippians 1:1-2; 4:10-20 is a note sent to the Philippian Christians thanking them for a gift of money that they had sent to Paul in prison. Philippians 1:3-3:1; 4:4-9 is a letter in which Paul reflects on his suffering, especially his present suffering in prison. In this letter he expresses a joyful confidence that whatever happens to him will serve the good of the gospel (Phil 1:19-26). Part of a third letter is found in Philippians 3:2-4:3. This letter is very different in tone from the other two. Paul once again is forced to oppose Jewish Christian missionaries who were preaching the necessity of Christian observance of the Mosaic Law (Phil 3:3-6). Paul emphasizes that observance of the Mosaic Law compromises the Christian's belief that true righteousness comes through faith in Christ (Phil 3:2-11).

After Paul had written his letter of reconciliation to the Corinthian Christians in the summer of A.D. 55, he also wrote two further letters (2 Cor 8 and 9) urging the Christians of Corinth and Achaia to complete their work on the collection for the poor of the Jerusalem Church. In order to complete this work, Paul himself came to Corinth and stayed there for approximately three months during the winter of A.D. 55-56.

At his meeting with the leaders of the Christian community at Jerusalem in A.D. 48, Paul had promised to remember the poor of the Jerusalem Church and take up a collection for them among the Christians with whom he was working (Gal 2:10). This collection involved all of the Christian communities in Greece and Asia Minor (see 2 Cor 9:2-5; 1 Cor 16:1), and Paul was now trying to bring it to completion.

It is crucial to keep in mind that this collection was not simply a matter of helping the "poor" of the Jerusalem community. It also involved trying to cement the relationship between Jewish and Gentile Christianity. What was at stake was the unity of these very different Christian communities. Paul's concern over the successful completion of the collection is reflected in the number of times that he mentions the collection in his letters (1 Cor 16:1–4; 2 Cor 8–9; Rom 15:26).

But his concern was not only that the money be successfully collected from the Gentile Christian communities; it was also that the collection be accepted by the Jerusalem community. After all, Paul had bitterly opposed the Jewish Christian missionaries who had come to Galatia from the Jerusalem community and preached the necessity of Christian observance of the Mosaic Law. In addition, much of the opposition that Paul had encountered during his missionary journeys had come from Jewish Christian missionaries of various sorts who had, in one form or another, preached that even Gentile Christians should observe the Mosaic Law. He had good reason, then, to worry whether the collection that he was taking up would even be accepted by the Jewish community of Jerusalem (Rom 15:30-33).

This concern may have been one of the principal reasons why Paul wrote his letter to the Christian community at Rome during his last stay at Corinth in the winter of A.D. 55-56. Paul tells the Roman Christians of his plans to visit Rome and of his hopes that they will support him in his plans to travel from Rome to Spain (Rom 15:24, 28). But before coming to Rome, Paul is careful to mention that he must first go to Jerusalem with the collection. He emphasizes that, because the Gentiles have come to share in the spiritual blessing of Judaism, they ought to be of material help to the Jewish Christians of Jerusalem (Rom 15:27).

One of Paul's motivations in writing the letter to the

Roman Christians may have been to enlist their help in prevailing on the Jerusalem community to accept the collection that Paul had taken up. The Christian community of Rome, because of its location in the capital city of the empire, was obviously an important and influential community. In addition, it seems to have been a community which had a strong Jewish Christian influence in it.

In order to gain the support of that important Christian community for the collection, Paul explains in detail those elements of his theology which were most controversial. He is at pains to show that the equality of Jews and Gentiles is grounded in traditionally Jewish interpretations of the Scriptures (Rom 1–3), that salvation apart from observance of the Mosaic Law has a precedent in the figure of Abraham (Rom 4), that the Mosaic Law itself is good (Rom 7), that non-observance of the Mosaic Law does not lead to gross immorality (Rom 5–6), and that, finally and most importantly, his preaching of the universality of the gospel does not ultimately lead to a rejection of the validity of God's promises to the Jews (Rom 8-11).

Jerusalem and Rome

Paul's letter to the Romans contains the last information that we have of Paul's life from his own letters. From this point on we have only the information provided by the Acts of the Apostles (Acts 20:7–28:31). Much of this information is probably legendary, especially the speeches before Jewish and Roman officials. But the accounts in Acts do give us some reliable information about what happened to Paul in Jerusalem and the causes of his final arrest and transfer to Rome.

In the spring of A.D. 56 Paul, accompanied by a delegation of fellow Christians, left Corinth and set off on their journey to Jerusalem with the collection. Rather than sailing directly to Palestine, they traveled first through northern Greece and then by stages along the coast of Asia Minor until they reached Caesarea on the coast of Palestine. The purpose of this route was probably twofold. First, it enabled Paul to visit Christian communities along the way and pick up their contributions to the collection. Second, this route was probably safer than making a direct voyage across the Mediterranean Sea to Palestine.

Paul and his delegation probably arrived in Jerusalem sometime late in the spring of A.D. 56. In Jerusalem Paul received an ambiguous reception. On the one hand, Acts 21:17-20 claims that Paul was given a warm welcome by James and the other leaders of the Jewish Christian community in Jerusalem. On the other hand, these leaders expressed their concern that many of the Jewish Christians would be scandalized by Paul's presence in Jerusalem, since he preached belief in Christ without the observance of the Mosaic Law (Acts 21:20-21). James and the elders suggested that Paul allay their fears by ritually purifying himself, going to the Temple, and paying the expenses for four men who had taken a Nazirite vow (Acts 21:23-24). Paul agreed to this measure. But when he went to the Temple, some Jews of Asia Minor who were aware of his reputation seized him, dragged him out of the Temple and threatened to kill him. When the Roman authorities heard of this, they came, arrested Paul, and put him in protective custody.

Because of a continuing plot against Paul, the Roman

tribune eventually sent him down to the Roman procurator Felix in Caesarea (Acts 23:12-35). Felix, who was known for his corruption, kept him in prison for two years (A.D. 56-58). In A.D. 58 Felix was replaced by Porcius Festus. Paul then appealed his case to Caesar and as a consequence was sent by Porcius Festus to Rome.

The journey to Rome, as it is described in Acts 27:1–28:16, including a shipwreck, contains much that is probably legendary. Paul probably arrived in Rome in early A.D. 59. Acts 28:30 claims that Paul was under house arrest in Rome for two years (A.D. 59-60). At this point the account of Paul's life in the Acts of the Apostles comes to an end. The next mention that we have of Paul comes from 1 Clement 5.5-7 (written in Rome ca. A.D. 96). This account presupposes that Paul was martyred in Rome. According to Jerome (*De viris illustribus 5*), Paul was beheaded on the Via Ostiensis. This may have occurred in A.D. 60-61.

When one looks at Paul's life, one is struck by his immense energy and commitment, first as a Pharisee and then as a believer in Jesus. He was obviously someone whose convictions were immediately transferred into commitment and action. His convictions were immediately reflected in his life.

One is also struck by the central role played by his own experiences. His own experience on the road to Damascus turned his life around and changed its direction forever. Although deeply rooted in the traditions of early Christianity, his own experiences as a missionary also played a formative role in his preaching and in the way that he understood and lived out his commitment as a believer in Christ.

Finally one is struck by the important role that both community and circumstances played in the formation of his theology and spirituality. Paul's letters to the various Christian communities scattered around the Mediterranean Sea were not theological treatises. Rather, they were attempts to deal with particular problems in particular communities. The circumstances in which these communities found themselves played a formative role in Paul's religious outlook. It was not as if Paul catered to their whims. Quite the contrary, he was often in conflict with them. But he always felt that it was crucial to appeal to their own experience of the Gospel, to try to understand that experience and to help them to understand it in a deeper and more complete way.

When one tries, then, to understand Paul's spirituality, one always has to be aware that it was limited by time and place and circumstance. Yet those limitations ultimately do not detract from Paul's significance for contemporary Christians. If a spirituality is not relevant for its own particular time and place and circumstance, it will never be relevant for any other time or place or circumstance. No spirituality is timeless; it is a real spirituality only if it is timely.

2

CALL OR CONVERSION

If one knows anything about the life of Paul, one probably knows the story of his "conversion" on the road to Damascus. The story was told three times by Luke in the Acts of the Apostles (9:1-19; 22:3-21; 26:2-18). Paul himself wrote about this experience and its significance in Galatians 1:11-17 and in 1 Corinthians 15:1-11. As we shall see, Paul certainly saw this experience on the road to Damascus as the one which changed his life forever.

Conversion or Call

Yet we must be careful when we speak of this crucial experience in Paul's life as a "conversion." The word "conversion" has several different meanings. For example, when we speak of a religious conversion, of someone "converting to Christianity" or "converting to Judaism," we usually mean that a person has either changed religions, that is, converted from one religion to another, or changed from unbelief to belief. We can also speak of a "moral conversion." Here we mean a change from a life of immorality to one of morality.

Yet Paul's experience on the road to Damascus was neither a religious nor a moral conversion in the usual sense of those terms. Paul certainly did not think of himself as an immoral person prior to what happened to him on the road to Damascus. On the contrary, he felt that he had been, if anything, a more observant Jew than most of his contemporaries. This is how Paul described his own life prior to his experience on the road to Damascus:

> 4If any other man thinks he has reason for confidence in the flesh, I have more: 5circumcised on the eighth day, of the people of Israel, of the tribe of Benjamin, a Hebrew born of Hebrews; as to the law a Pharisee, 6as to zeal a persecutor of the church, as to righteousness under the law blameless. (Phil 3:4-6)

His practice of the Mosaic Law in his own mind was blameless. Even if one allows for a certain amount of rhetorical exaggeration in the passage from Philippians, Paul still did not see the experience on the road to Damascus as a moral conversion.

Nor did Paul ever interpret his experience as a religious conversion, that is, as a change from unbelief to belief or as a change from one religion to another. Paul never spoke of "leaving" Judaism to become something else, that is, a Christian. As we shall see, Paul's relationship to his fellow Jews and to Judaism was complex; nevertheless, he never speaks of his commitment to Christ as a change of religion. Rather he saw his commitment to Christ as a fulfillment of his own commitment to Judaism and to Judaism's God.

If what happened to Paul on the road to Damascus was not

a conversion, what then was it? To answer this question we must look at the Letter to the Galatians where Paul gives us his own account of this experience.

> [11]For I would have you know, brethren, that the gospel which was preached by me is not man's gospel. [12]For I did not receive it from man nor was I taught it, but it came through a revelation of Jesus Christ. [13]For you have heard of my former life in Judaism, how I persecuted the church of God violently and tried to destroy it; [14]and I advanced in Judaism beyond many of my own age among my people, so extremely zealous was I for the traditions of my fathers. [15]But when he who had set me apart before I was born, and had called me through his grace, [16]was pleased to reveal his Son to me, in order that I might preach him among the Gentiles, I did not confer with flesh and blood, [17]nor did I go up to Jerusalem to those who were apostles before me, but I went away into Arabia; and again I returned to Damascus. (Gal 1:11-17)

Paul describes his experience on the road to Damascus as a "revelation" and as a "call," but not as a "conversion." When he describes for his Galatian readers his "former life in Judaism," he is not trying to say that he is no longer a Jew but that his practice of Judaism has radically changed since his experience of the risen Lord on the road to Damascus. The images that he uses to describe this experience are drawn from the calls of Israelite prophets, especially from the calls of Jeremiah and Isaiah.

In Galatians 1:15-16 where Paul actually describes his initial experience, he claims that he was set apart before he was born and that, when God was pleased to reveal his Son to him, it was in order that he preach him among the Gentiles. The images both of God calling the prophet from his mother's womb and speaking to the Gentiles are found in Isaiah 49:1, 5–6:

> [1]The Lord called me from the womb,
>   from the body of my mother he named my name . . .
> [5]And now the Lord says,
>   who formed me from the womb to be his servant,
> to bring Jacob back to him,
>   and that Israel might be gathered to him,
> for I am honored in the eyes of the Lord,
>   and my God has become my strength—
> [6]he says:
> "It is too light a thing that you should be my servant,
>   to raise up the tribes of Jacob,
>   and to restore the preserved of Israel;
> I will give you as a light to the nations,
>   that my salvation may reach to the end of the earth."

This quotation from Second Isaiah contains two motifs central to Paul's own call. The first is the motif of being called by God before birth, while still in his mother's womb. The second motif is that the prophet is sent not only to Israel but is also sent to be a "light to the nations." One must remember that the Hebrew word used in Isaiah 49:6 means both "nations" and "Gentiles."

These same two motifs are found even more clearly in the story of the call of the prophet Jeremiah.

> "Before I (God) formed you in the womb I knew you,
>   and before you were born I consecrated you;
>   I appointed you a prophet to the nations." (Jer 1:5)

Here again, as in Isaiah, Jeremiah is called before he was born to prophesy to the Gentiles. In addition, this section of Jeremiah is Jeremiah's initial, inaugural vision and in that way closely parallels Paul's own initial vision.

Undoubtedly Isaiah and Jeremiah meant something different by being "a light to the nations" or "a prophet to the nations" than Paul did by "preaching among the Gentiles." Nevertheless, these central motifs drawn by Paul from Isaiah and Jeremiah indicate that Paul understood this experience not as a "conversion" but as a "prophetic call." In other words, the same God whom he had worshipped before his call now called him to preach to the Gentiles.

The call of each prophet, of course, was unique regarding precisely what he was called to preach. The oracles of Isaiah differed from those of Jeremiah. In his case, Paul was called upon to preach Christ, the Son whom God had revealed to him. It was this revelation that brought about not a conversion but certainly a radical change in Paul's life.

Up until the time of his call, Paul, as he described himself in Galatians 1:13-14, both persecuted the church of God violently and was extremely zealous for the traditions of his fathers, that is, for the observance of the Mosaic Law according to the Pharisaic sect to which he claimed to belong (cf. Phil 3:5). Paul's call, then, represented a fundamental reversal of two crucial convictions central to his previous way of life. In the first place, the Jesus whose followers Paul had persecuted was revealed to him as God's Son by God himself. Secondly, his call to preach this Son to the Gentiles led him to radically reevaluate the status of the Mosaic Law to which he had previously been so committed. It is important to notice that in Galatians 1:13-14 Paul lists those two crucial aspects of his life which were turned upside-down in the experience of his call.

Paul, then, understood this initial experience which so changed his life as a prophetic call, rather than as what we think of as a religious or moral conversion. He did not think of this call to preach Christ to the Gentiles as a desertion of Judaism or of Judaism's God. Quite the contrary, it was Judaism's God whom he experienced as calling him to preach Christ to the Gentiles.

Yet there are two aspects of Paul's experience which do go beyond what one usually thinks of as a call, which look more like what one thinks of as a conversion. The first aspect is the extent to which Paul's experience altered some of his most deeply held convictions. As I mentioned above, Paul's life prior to his call was deeply informed by his commitment to the observance of the Mosaic Law and by his conviction that those who believed in Jesus were unfaithful to Judaism. These two fundamental convictions changed or, better, were changed by Paul's experience on the road to Damascus, by his encounter with the risen Lord. Prophetic calls, such as those of Isaiah and Jeremiah, did not involve such changes in fundamental convictions or commitments. They certainly involved a change in the prophet's way of life, but not a change in his fundamental convictions. In that sense, Paul was changed in a way that the prophets were not.

Paul's experience also went beyond what one usually thinks of as a call in a second sense. As we shall see, one of Paul's fundamental convictions, rooted in his experience on the road to Damascus, came to be that the observance of the Mosaic Law was no longer obligatory for those who believed in Christ. Paul saw that conviction as compatible with his commitment to the God of Judaism. Yet, the conviction that the observance of the Mosaic Law was no longer obligatory was one of the fundamental causes for the eventual separation of Christianity from Judaism, for the development of Christianity into a new and distinct religion. The consequences, then, of Paul's call, although not his own experience of it, involved elements of what we normally think of as the consequences of a conversion, that is, the movement from one religion to another. Thus, while Paul's own interpretation of his experience is one of call, there are aspects of that call, the radical alteration of fundamental convictions and the consequences of that alteration, which, in retrospect, give the appearances of a conversion.

Two Views of Paul's Call

There are several other aspects of Paul's call that help us to understand how Paul saw his own identity and his work as a missionary. These aspects are best understood by comparing Paul's own description and interpretation of his call with the description and interpretation given by Luke in the Acts of the Apostles.

The author of the Acts of the Apostles narrated the story of Paul's call three times (Acts 9:1-19; 22:3-21; 26:2-18). The first version is a third-person narrative, and the second and third are first-person narratives spoken by Paul himself. The fullest version and the one most helpful for our purposes is the one found in Acts 9:1-19.

According to this version, Paul received letters from the high priest in Jerusalem to the synagogues of Damascus which would allow him to bind and bring to Jerusalem any followers of Jesus whom he might find in Damascus. In the first scene (Acts 9:1-9), as he and his fellow travelers were approaching Damascus, a light flashed from heaven and Paul fell to the ground. He then heard a voice saying to him: "Saul, Saul, why do you persecute me?" Paul asked who was speaking, and the voice replied that it was Jesus whom Paul had been persecuting. The voice then told him to go into Damascus where he would be told what he was to do. When Paul got up from the ground, he was blind and so had to be led by his fellow travelers into Damascus.

The second scene (Acts 9:10-16) takes place in Damascus, at the house of a Jewish Christian by the name of Ananias. In this scene Ananias had a vision of the Lord in which he was told to go to a certain house and there to lay hands on Paul so that he might receive back his sight. Ananias was also told that Paul had had a parallel vision in which he saw Ananias coming to lay hands on him. Ananias protested that Paul had a reputation for persecuting the followers of Jesus. But Ananias was told by the Lord to go to Paul for he "is a chosen instrument of mine to carry my name before the Gentiles and kings and the sons of Israel" (Acts 9:15).

In the third and final scene (Acts 9:17-19), Ananias arrived at the house where Paul was staying. Ananias then told Paul that the Lord whom he encountered on the road to Damascus had sent him. He then laid his hands on Paul, and Paul regained his sight and was filled with the Holy Spirit.

When compared with what Paul himself said about his experience on the way to Damascus, the story as it is narrated in Acts 9 is far more detailed. A number of the details, such as Paul's commission to the synagogues of Damascus and the parallel visions of Paul and Ananias, may be legendary. Nevertheless, those details give us clues about how the author of the Acts of the Apostles understood Paul's role in the history of early Christianity.

Both Paul and the account in Acts 9 agree that prior to this point, Paul persecuted the followers of Jesus (Acts 9:1-2; Gal 1:13-14). Both also agree on the fact that Paul's overpowering experience of Christ took place on the way to Damascus. Finally, both agree that Paul had a crucial role to play in preaching to the Gentiles. Yet their interpretations of that experience differ considerably, and those differences highlight how Paul's understanding of his identity and role differed from the way in which that identity and role were interpreted two generations later by Luke in the Acts of the Apostles.

The first major difference between Paul's account in Galatians and the narrative in Acts 9 has to do with the nature of the experience itself. In Acts 9, Paul sees a light from heaven and hears the voice of Jesus calling to him. But he does not see Jesus, that is, Jesus does not appear to him; nor, at first, does Paul recognize the voice. Luke in Acts 9 is careful not to describe Paul's experience in the same way that he described the appearances of Jesus to various disciples after the resurrection where the disciples see Jesus (Luke 24:1-52).

In Paul's own account, however, we are led to believe that when God revealed his Son to Paul (Gal 1:16), Paul actually "saw" Jesus. This impression is strengthened by passages from both 1 Corinthians and 2 Corinthians. In 1 Corinthians 15:5-8, Paul gives a traditional list of people to whom the risen Jesus appeared. The last one to whom he appeared, "as to one untimely born," was Paul himself. In other words, Jesus appeared to Paul in the same way that he had previously appeared to Peter, to the twelve, to James, etc. Paul saw the risen Lord in the same way as the other disciples did. In 2 Corinthians 12:2-5, Paul describes another religious experience, one which took place sometime after his initial one on the road to Damascus. In this experience he is caught up into the third heaven and hears things that cannot be told. Once again, there is a strong visionary element. Paul, then, understood his experience on the road to Damascus as one in which the risen Lord appeared to him.

These two different accounts of Paul's experience on the road to Damascus point to two very different evaluations. For Luke, what happened to Paul on the road to Damascus was *not* to be counted among the "appearances of the risen Lord to his apostles." For the author of the Acts of the Apostles, that kind of appearance ended at the ascension of Jesus (Luke 24:50-52; Acts 1:6-11). For Luke, Jesus appeared to the apostles during the forty days after his resurrection and spoke to them about the Kingdom of God (Acts 1:2-3). But that privileged period ended with the ascension. After that, Jesus' disciples experienced his presence among them, sometimes in very profound ways, as in the case of Paul; but these experiences were technically not to be counted among the privileged "appearances of the risen Lord."

Paul, however, understood his experience quite differently. For him, it was an appearance of the risen Lord, the same kind of experience had by Peter and the other apostles. In this way, Paul placed his own initial experience on the same level, in the same privileged position as the appearances to the other first disciples.

These different evaluations of the status of Paul's initial experience of the risen Lord also led to different evaluations of Paul's status within the early Christian community. Paul himself insisted that he was an apostle. He began his letter to the Galatians, both letters to the Corinthians, and his letter to the Romans with a reference to the fact that he had been called to be an apostle. Paul grounded his claim to be an apostle in his experience of the risen Lord. This emerges most clearly in 1 Corinthians 15:8-11, a passage in which Paul interpreted the appearance of the risen Lord to him described in Galatians 1:11-17:

> [8]Last of all, as to one untimely born, he appeared also to me. [9]For I am the least of the apostles, unfit to be called an apostle, because I persecuted the church of God. [10]But by the grace of God I am what I am, and his grace towards me was not in vain. On the contrary, I worked harder than any of them, though it was not I but the grace of God which is with me. [11]Whether then it was I or they, so we preach and so you believed.

Paul's claim is that because the risen Lord had appeared to him just as he appeared to Peter, James, and the other apostles, Paul had the right to be numbered among the apostles. It is also obvious from this passage in 1 Corinthians 15 that Paul's claim to be an apostle had not gone unchallenged. While ingenuously admitting that he is the least of the apostles, even unfit to be called an apostle because he persecuted the church, Paul goes on to claim that he is what he is by the grace of God and that he has worked harder than any of the other apostles, all of course by the grace of God. He is clearly defending himself against the charge that he is not really an apostle, that is, that he is not really on the same level as the first disciples of Jesus who were witnesses to Jesus' resurrection. For Paul, then, the experience on the road to Damascus not only radically changed his way of life and some of his fundamental religious convictions, it also gave him legitimacy in the Christian community as an apostle and put him on a par with the other leaders of the Christian community, especially the other leaders of the Christian community in Jerusalem.

The author of the Acts of the Apostles, however, does not see Paul as an apostle. Except for a passing reference in Acts 14:14 to Paul and Barnabas as "apostles," Luke reserves the title of apostle to a much more limited group of disciples. For him the title "apostle" is restricted to the twelve disciples who were called by Jesus to be apostles (see Luke 6:13) and whose number was reestablished when Matthias was chosen by lot to replace Judas (Acts 1:26). In the story of the choosing of Matthias, Luke's criteria for being an apostle emerge quite clearly:

> [21]So one of the men who have accompanied us during all the time that the Lord Jesus went in and out among us, [22]beginning from the baptism of John until the day when he was taken up from us—one of these men must become with us a witness to his resurrection. (Acts 1:21-22)

For Luke an apostle was a member of the very small group who were with Jesus from the beginning of his public ministry and served as official witnesses to his resurrection, that is, to whom Jesus appeared after his resurrection but prior to his ascension. Given the fact that this group as a group does very little throughout the rest of the Acts of the Apostles, its main function in Luke's mind seems to have been to serve as a link between the earthly and resurrected Jesus and the beginnings of the Christian Church. They served to link together the period of Jesus and the period of the Church. For Luke, Paul plays no such role and so is not numbered among the apostles.

In Luke's eyes, then, Paul does not belong to the first generation of disciples, that is, to the generation of the apostles, but to the second generation. In fact, for Luke, Paul's mission to the Gentiles is finally legitimated only at the meeting at

Jerusalem in A.D. 48. At that meeting described in Acts
15:1-29, the apostles along with the elders (Acts 15: 2, 4, 6, 22,
23) give final approval to Paul's mission to the Gentiles by
deciding that Gentile Christians did not have to observe most
of the Mosaic Law.

This interpretation, of course, would have been quite
unacceptable to Paul, for Paul felt that his preaching to the
Gentiles without demanding observance of the Mosaic Law
was grounded not in any human authority but in the revelation of Jesus Christ in his experience on the road to Damascus
(Gal 1:11-12). Luke, on the other hand, saw Paul as someone
whose authority was derived from the apostles in Jerusalem.
Just as the apostles were a link between the period of Jesus and
the period of the Church, Paul was a link, within the period of
the Church, between the first generation, represented by the
apostles in Jerusalem, and the third generation, the largely
Gentile churches to which Luke belonged. For Luke, Paul was
the great missionary to the Gentiles but he was not an apostle;
his legitimacy and authority were derived from the generation
of the apostles and he passed that legitimacy and authority on
to the next generation, the generation of the Gentile churches
to which Luke belonged (Acts 20:17-38).

A third major difference between Paul's own understanding of his experience on the road to Damascus and Luke's
understanding of that same experience concerns the way in
which the call to preach to the Gentiles was received. As Luke
tells the story in Acts 9, the voice of Jesus which Paul heard on
the road outside of Damascus told him, "I am Jesus, whom
you are persecuting; but rise and enter the city, and you will be
told what you are to do" (Acts 9:5-6). While Paul was staying
in Damascus, waiting to regain his sight and to be told what he

was to do, the Lord appeared to Ananias, a Jewish Christian living in Damascus, and told Ananias: "Go, for he (Paul) is a chosen instrument of mine to carry my name before the Gentiles and kings and the sons of Israel" (Acts 9:15). Paul did not receive his commission to preach to the Gentiles in the revelation itself. Rather, the commission was communicated to him indirectly through a vision given to Ananias. What this means is that Paul received his commission to preach to the Gentiles through the mediation of someone who was already a member of the Christian community.

Paul's own interpretation of the experience, however, is quite different. In his mind, the commission to preach to the Gentiles was not mediated through the Christian community but was an integral part of his experience on the road to Damascus.

> [15]But when he who had set me apart before I was born, and had called me through his grace, [16]was pleased to reveal his Son to me, in order to preach him among the Gentiles, I did not confer with flesh and blood, [17]nor did I go up to Jerusalem to those who were apostles before me, but I went away into Arabia; and again I returned to Damascus. (Gal 1:15-17).

According to Paul he was not told of his mission to the Gentiles by Ananias or by any other member of the Christian community. That commission was given to him by God himself in his revelation to Paul. Paul is insistent on that fact. Not even after the revelation on the road to Damascus did Paul go up to Jerusalem to meet with "those who were apostles" before him. For Paul, the gospel he was preaching was not a human gospel nor was it received from human sources.

[11]For I would have you know brethren, that the gospel which was preached by me is not man's gospel. [12]For I did not receive it from man, nor was I taught it, but it came through a revelation of Jesus Christ. (Gal 1:11-12)

Paul then goes on to admit that three years later he did go up to Jerusalem to visit with Peter and James (Gal 1:18-19); but he carefully describes that meeting as a visit and not an admission on his part that he needed their approval for the legitimacy of his mission to the Gentiles.

This difference between Luke and Paul about how Paul received his commission to preach to the Gentiles once again brings out a fundamental difference between the two about Paul's identity and function within early Christianity. Luke is at pains to place Paul within a larger context of continuity in the development of early Christianity. Paul receives his commission within the context of the developing Christian community. He is integrated into a relatively conflict-free development of the mission of that community to the Gentiles.

For Paul, however, the situation is quite different. He grounds his own preaching to the Gentiles not in a commission that he received from the Christian community but in revelation of Jesus Christ that he received from God himself. Paul's own polemical insistence on this fact is undoubtedly related to the situation that he was dealing with in his Letter to the Galatians. In that letter he seems to be dealing with Christian communities who had come to be influenced by Jewish-Christian missionaries, probably from Jerusalem, who claimed that Christians, whether ethnically Jewish or Gentile, had to observe the Mosaic Law. In addition, they seem to have claimed that the legitimacy of Paul's preaching could come only from the authority of the Jerusalem community and that they, and not Paul, had that legitimacy. In order to counteract their position, Paul insisted that, while his preaching to the Gentiles without demanding observance of the Mosaic Law was accepted by the Jerusalem community (Gal 2:7-9), that preaching was not grounded in their acceptance but rather their acceptance was grounded in the fact that he had received his commission from a revelation of Jesus Christ by God himself. Paul, unlike Luke, did not see himself as a link within the continuity of the development of the early Christian community but as an independent source of authority whose legitimacy was not derived from the approval of the Christian community in Jerusalem but from a revelation of God himself.

Conclusion

We have spent a good deal of time analyzing Paul's own account of his experience on the road to Damascus and comparing it with the account given by Luke in Acts 9. In a sense, the reasons for this are obvious. First, Paul himself saw this experience as the crucial turning point in his life. It changed his life forever. Second, by comparing Paul's interpretation of this experience with that of Luke, we gain a sense of how Paul understood himself in relationship to other early Christians, and how he grounded his legitimacy as an apostle in that experience.

There is, however, a third and for our purposes most important reason for analyzing Paul's experience on the road to Damascus so closely. Paul's spirituality and his theology are rooted in his own Christian experience. That did not mean that the traditions of the early Church about Jesus were unimportant to Paul. Quite the contrary, he took them quite seriously and frequently made use of them. Nevertheless, he interpreted those traditions in the light of his own experience of Christ on the road to Damascus. As we shall see, his emphasis on the universality of Christ, on the end of the Mosaic Law, and on the inclusion of the Gentiles were all rooted in this central experience of his life. This experience, then, did not simply change *his* life but, in the process, also changed the direction of a significant segment of early Christianity. He is, perhaps, the prime example of how religious experience can creatively and permanently change the direction of a religious tradition.

3

PAUL'S EXPERIENCE OF
GOD AND CHRIST

Paul's experience on the road to Damascus was certainly one of the central experiences of his life. It changed the direction of his life forever. The one who had at first been a persecutor of Christians now became one of Christianity's missionaries. Yet this experience was not simply an isolated phenomenon. Paul's experience on the road to Damascus was surrounded by Paul's larger religious convictions, convictions about who God was and what God's relationship to humankind was all about. Paul's convictions on these matters were rooted in the Judaism of the period and those convictions never left Paul. In addition, Paul's convictions as a Christian were profoundly influenced by the traditional beliefs and practices of the Christianity of which he became a part. Paul's vision of God and of Christ, then, was formed by the interaction of his Jewish beliefs about God and his experience on the road to Damascus.

Put in a different way, Paul's vision of God and of Christ was marked by the interaction of tradition and experience.

This interaction formed the basis for his religious sensibilities, much as our own religious sensibilities are formed by that same interaction. All of us are born into a world that is already formed by various outlooks, whether religious or secular. We do not create the world into which we are born. Rather, as we grow up, we internalize the outlooks of that world. This process of internalization goes on almost unnoticed. We grow up in a world whose viewpoints and attitudes seem quite natural to us, almost as obvious and as unnoticed as the air we breathe. We grow into and become part of that world.

Yet our basic outlooks and attitudes are not simply a mirror image of that world. The process of internalization is filtered through our own experience. Granted that the world forms our experience to a great extent, it does not completely determine it. To some extent at least, each of us has his or her own particular perspective on the world. In other words, our own experience also plays a crucial role in forming the way in which we live and understand the world around us. We, too, are formed by both tradition and experience.

I would like to explore in this chapter the way in which Paul's religious sensibilities were formed by the interaction between the religious traditions of which Paul was a part and his own experience. In a very fundamental sense, this is what one means by a spirituality, a person's basic convictions, attitudes, and sensibilities about God and the relationship of God to the world.

Tradition

A central, formative element in Paul's religious outlook was the Judaism into which he was born and in which he grew up. He himself emphasizes his own commitment to Judaism in Philippians 3:5-6 and again in 2 Corinthians 12:22. He was a Hebrew, an Israelite, circumcised on the eighth day, and a committed member of the Pharisaic sect of Judaism. As a committed Jew he had certain deeply held religious convictions. His most basic conviction was belief in only one God, his belief in Jewish monotheism. In 1 Thessalonians 1:9-10 he describes for the Thessalonian Christians their own conversion to Christianity. They turned from idols to serve a living and true God. In a similar vein he chides the Galatian Christians for, in his mind, trying to turn once again from God to serve the beggarly elemental spirits of the universe, that is, pagan idols (Gal 4:9-10). Before they came to know God they were in bondage to beings who by nature were not gods (Gal 4:8). For Paul, as for other Jews, there was only one God.

All other beings who laid claim to being gods were "beggarly elemental spirits" (Gal 4:9). These were the idols of the Graeco-Roman world. For Paul, as for many Jews of the period, these elemental spirits did exist and they did have power over much of what happened in the world. Yet they were not divine; they were not God. Their power could not rival that of God. Rather, they were "fallen angels" who had chosen to be disobedient. Often enough they were understood as powers which inhabited the heavenly bodies and through those heavenly bodies, they had an influence on the world below, an influence that was direful. For Paul, the pagan world worshipped those elemental spirits as if they really were gods, and by worshipping them they were in bondage to them. The world was a place of conflict, a conflict in which Paul was certain that God would be victorious over these elemental spirits, but it still was a place of conflict. By turning to Judaism and belief in Christ, one was freed from that bondage. It is of this that he was reminding the Galatian Christians.

A second and equally important conviction that Paul derived from Judaism was his belief that this one God revealed himself in the Hebrew Scriptures. Throughout his letters Paul quotes from the Hebrew Scriptures as writings inspired and revealed by God. As his arguments based on those scriptures show, Paul believed that they formed a seamless garment. There were no inconsistencies in them, and every word of them conveyed some important meaning.

Central to these scriptures was the Mosaic Law, the Torah. Throughout his life Paul defended the value and the revealed character of the Mosaic Law. He also argued that in Christ the Mosaic Law had come to an end. Yet he always maintained that the Mosaic Law was good. It was meant to last for only a limited time, and it reached its goal in the coming of Christ. He even argued that the end of the Mosaic Law in Christ was predicted by the Law itself. By arguing in that way, Paul broke with the viewpoint of most of the Jews of his own time. Nevertheless, in his mind, his arguments for the end of the practice of the Mosaic Law were arguments that he derived from the Hebrew Scriptures themselves. Paul's Bible always remained the Bible of Judaism.

Paul's religious sensibilities were also deeply influenced by the traditions of the Christianity of which he became a part. As a persecutor of Christians prior to his call or conversion, Paul was probably familiar with basic Christian beliefs. Prior to his call he obviously found those beliefs objectionable but was, for that very reason, familiar with at least some of the more central beliefs of those whom he was so intent on persecuting. After his call those same beliefs became his central convictions also.

First among those beliefs was certainly the centrality of Christ. It is not altogether clear how much Paul knew of the traditional stories and sayings of Jesus. What is clear is that Paul found the central message of his new-found faith in the crucifixion, death, and resurrection of Christ. Even though he may have known some of the traditions about Jesus' activities and sayings, his primary concern was with the death and resurrection of Jesus.

More specifically, when Paul seems to be using traditional Christian material about Jesus' death and resurrection, he draws heavily on early Christian interpretations of Jesus' death and resurrection which used sacrificial metaphors. An example of this is found in Romans 3:21-26.

> [21]But now the righteousness of God has been revealed apart from law, although the law and the prophets bear witness to it, [22]the righteousness of God through faith in Jesus Christ for all who believe. For there is no distinction; [23]since all have sinned and fall short of the glory of God, [24]they are justified by his grace as a gift through the redemption which is in Jesus Christ, [25]whom God put forward as an expiation by his blood, to be received by faith. This was to show God's righteousness, because in his divine forbearance he has passed over former sins; [26]it was to prove at the present time that he himself is righteous and that he justifies him who has faith in Jesus.

Paul's viewpoint on the Law and justification apart from the Law was Paul's own. But his description of Jesus' death as an expiatory sacrifice was traditional Christian language used to interpret Jesus' crucifixion, death, and resurrection. The point of such language was not to portray an angry God who was demanding reparation from a sinful people. Rather the point of the imagery was to portray a merciful God who, in the "sacrifice" of Jesus, was reconciling sinful humanity to himself.

A second traditional Christian viewpoint that always remained central for Paul was the belief in Jesus' future coming in power. Throughout his letters, Paul reflects the early Christian belief that Jesus will soon return in power. This belief will be important not only for Paul's Christology but also for his ethics and for the advice that he will offer the Christian communities which he had a hand in founding.

The Experience of Power

Yet if many of Paul's beliefs were derived either from Judaism or from early Christian tradition, his own experience of God and of Christ led him to interpret those traditional beliefs in new ways and to give them different emphases. There is an interaction between tradition and experience.

In order to understand how that interaction worked in the case of Paul, one has to understand as best one can from this distance Paul's own basic metaphors for understanding reality. All of us have basic strategies for dealing with ourselves and with the world around us. Some of us see the world as something to be understood or contemplated. Others see it as a reality to be overcome, to be conquered. Still others see the world as a reality to be feared, something to be protected from.

These basic strategies influence all of our particular viewpoints and decisions. Put another way, each of us is guided by root paradigms or root metaphors. By that I mean those basic concepts, images, and symbols by which we guide our lives, those elementary motifs to which we turn in times of crises for understanding and guidance.

The same was true for Paul. In his case those root metaphors or paradigms clustered around the notion of power. Both before and after his call or conversion, Paul's images of God and of Christ were deeply influenced by those images of power.

At several points in his letters, Paul describes his life prior to his experience of Christ on the road to Damascus (Phil 3:4-6; Gal 1:13-14; 2 Cor 11:22). Although all of these notices are quite brief, they do give us a sense of how Paul saw his life prior to his call. The most helpful of these references is in Philippians 3:4-6:

> 4If any other man thinks he has reason for confidence in the flesh, I have more: 5circumcised on the eighth day, of the people of Israel, of the tribe of Benjamin, a Hebrew born of Hebrews, 6as to zeal a persecutor of the church, as to righteousness under the law blameless.

The context of this quotation is a polemic against Christians who were tempted to observe the Mosaic Law. Because of that Paul may have been exaggerating his own practice of Judaism a bit. Nevertheless this passage does give us a portrait of Paul as a man who had a firm sense of his own power, a man who successfully accomplished what he had set out to do. He was a Pharisee who zealously and successfully observed the commandments of the Mosaic Law and who in his zeal also persecuted those Jews who believed in Jesus.

After his call, Paul exudes that same sense of power. The most revealing passage in this regard is 2 Corinthians 11:23-28.

> [23]Are they servants of Christ? I am a better one—I am talking like a madman—with far greater labors, far more imprisonments, with countless beatings, and often near death. [24]Five times I have received at the hands of the Jews the forty lashes less one. [25]Three times I have been beaten with rods; once I was stoned. Three times I have been shipwrecked; a night and a day I have been adrift at sea; [26]on frequent journeys, in danger from rivers, danger from robbers, danger from my own people, danger from Gentiles, danger in the city, danger in the wilderness, danger at sea, danger from false brethren; [27]in toil and hardship, through many a sleepless night, in hunger and thirst, often without food, in cold and exposure. [28]And, apart from other things, there is the daily pressure upon me of my anxiety for all the churches.

Once again the context is very polemical; this time it is directed against other Christian missionaries who claim to be better than Paul. Once again Paul may be exaggerating. Yet the image that Paul gives of himself is important in understanding how Paul saw himself and his accomplishments. He saw himself as someone who was active and powerful, someone who accomplished his purposes regardless of the difficulties that he had to overcome to be successful.

One gets this sense of power throughout all of Paul's letters. As he uses his powers of persuasion, one has the very clear impression that Paul expected to be listened to and obeyed. He did not see his letters as simply helpful advice that his readers could take or leave as they saw best. Quite the contrary, he expected that the Christian communities to which he wrote would take his advice seriously and come to the same conclusions that he did.

The Experience of God

Because the root metaphor in Paul's life was power and because it influenced his own understanding of himself and of his relationship to the Christian communities that he founded, it could not but affect his own experience and understanding of God and his relationship to God. God, too, was understood in images of power.

This sense of the power of God comes out very clearly at the beginning of his Letter to the Romans. He asserts that he is not ashamed of the gospel that he is preaching, for "it is the power of God for salvation to every one who has faith, to the Jew first and also to the Greek" (Rom 1:16). A similar emphasis emerges several verses later when he indicts the Gentiles for not recognizing God from his works of creation.

> [20]Ever since the creation of the world his invisible nature, namely his eternal power and deity, has been clearly perceived in the things that have been made. So they are without excuse; [21]for although they knew God they did not honor him as God or give thanks to him but they became futile in their thinking and their senseless minds were darkened. (Rom 1:20-21)

When Paul sets out to describe God's "invisible nature," the first attribute that he settles on is his "eternal power."

This same view of God emerges even when Paul seems to be talking about something else. In 1 Corinthians 1–4 Paul is trying to persuade the Corinthian Christians that their claims to wisdom are unfounded. The context is one of claims and counterclaims about religious wisdom. Yet Paul alters the terms of the debate; he changes the terms to ones of power and weakness.

> [1]When I came to you, brethren, I did not come proclaiming to you the testimony of God in lofty words or wisdom. [2]For I decided to know nothing among you except Jesus Christ and him crucified. [3]And I was with you in weakness and in much fear and trembling; [4]and my speech and my message were not in plausible words of wisdom, but in demonstration of the Spirit and of power, [5]that your faith might not rest in the wisdom of men but in the power of God. (1 Cor 2:1-5)

While the Corinthian Christians saw their religious lives in terms of the wisdom that they now possessed as Christians, Paul saw his belief in terms of divine power and human weakness. In 1 Corinthians 2:5 Paul contrasts human wisdom not with the wisdom of God but with the power of God. Paul immediately goes on to claim that to the truly mature (not in his mind the Corinthian Christians) God does impart a certain kind of wisdom, yet it is very revealing that he roots that mature wisdom in the power of God. His almost unconscious response is to describe the Christian experience of God in terms of power.

The Experience of Christ

The same is true when Paul describes the Christian's experience of Christ. The most revealing passage in Paul's letters in this regard is again found in 1 Corinthians. Again Paul is trying to combat the Corinthian Christians' claim to the depths of religious wisdom.

> [18]For the word of the cross is folly to those who are perishing, but to us who are being saved it is the power of God. [19]For it is written, "I will destroy the wisdom of the wise, and the cleverness of the clever I will thwart" (Isa 29:14; Ps 33:10). [20]Where is the wise man? Where is the scribe? Where is the debater of this age? Has not God made foolish the wisdom of the world? [21]For since, in the wisdom of God, the world did not know God through wisdom, it pleased God through the folly of what we preach to save those who believe. [22]For Jews demand signs and Greeks seek wisdom, [23]but we preach Christ crucified, a stumbling block to Jews and folly to Gentiles, [24]but to those who are called, both Jews and Greeks, Christ the power of God and the wisdom of God. [25]For the foolishness of God is wiser than men, and the weakness of God is stronger than men. (1 Cor 1:18-25)

Paul again changes the terms of the debate. Instead of meeting the Corinthian Christians' claim head-on, he introduces new terms into the debate, ones of power and weakness. Christ becomes the way in which the "power of God and the wisdom of God" is revealed in the world, the way in which it is made manifest. The categories of wisdom and folly are still present, but they are now qualified and understood in a different way. What this points to is that Paul's first way to understand God and God's action in Christ in the world is through the notion of divine power.

Put in a slightly different way, God is understood as a realm of power and that power is now made present in the world through what God has done in Christ. That power is most clearly manifested in God's raising Jesus from the dead. Paul is willing to stake everything on that power, to count everything as loss because of the power of God manifested in the resurrection of Jesus.

> [8]Indeed I count everything as loss because of the surpassing worth of knowing Christ Jesus my Lord. For his sake I have suffered the loss of all things, and count them as refuse, in order that I may gain Christ [9]and be found in him, not having a righteousness of my own, based on law, but that which is through faith; [10]that I may know him and the power of his resurrection, and may share his sufferings, becoming like him in his death, [11]that if possible I may attain the resurrection from the dead. (Phil 3:8-11)

Paul is here opposing those Philippian Christians who want to observe the Mosaic Law. He wants to claim that Christian experience and belief is on a different plane. It is no longer the observance of the Mosaic Law that is central. In fact, in light of the Christian's experience of the risen Lord, everything else, including the Mosaic Law, is to be put aside. The power, then, that Paul experiences is the power of Jesus' resurrection; and it is that power that he firmly hopes will also be the power of his own resurrection. Nothing else can be of any value when compared to that power.

Paul sets this divine power that Christians experience through the resurrection of Christ over against other hostile powers. For Paul the world is an arena of conflict, a place where two different kinds of power are in competition. The first and, in Paul's mind, ultimately victorious power is that of God which has now been manifested in Christ and in his resurrection. The other power is that of the "weak and beggarly elemental spirits" (Gal 4:9). These elemental spirits are the demonic powers that control the universe apart from

God and Christ. Paul identifies these elemental spirits with the gods and goddesses of the Graeco-Roman world (Gal 4:9-10). They are the demonic powers that control the universe. In addition, they are the powers who were responsible for the crucifixion and death of Jesus.

> [7]But we impart a secret and hidden wisdom of God, which God decreed before the ages for our glorification. [8]None of the rulers of this age understood this; for if they had, they would not have crucified the Lord of glory. (1 Cor 2:7-8)

In this passage Paul means by the "rulers of this age" not Pilate, the Roman procurator, or the Jewish leaders but those heavenly, demonic powers who control the universe apart from God.

Paul's attitude toward these elemental spirits of the universe appears most clearly in his exhortation to the Corinthian Christians about the use of meat which had previously been offered to idols.

> [14]Therefore, my beloved, shun the worship of idols. [15]I speak as to sensible men; judge for yourselves what I say. [16]The cup of blessing which we bless, is it not a participation in the blood of Christ? The bread which we break, is it not a participation in the body of Christ? [17]Because there is one bread, we who are many are one body, for we all partake in the one bread.
> [18]Consider the people of Israel; are not those who eat the sacrifices partners in the altar? [19]What do I imply then? That food offered to idols is anything, or that an idol is anything? [20]No, I imply that what pagans sacrifice they offer to demons and not to God. I do not want you to be partners with demons. [21]You cannot drink the cup of the Lord and the cup of demons. You cannot partake of the table of the Lord and the table of demons. (1 Cor 10:14-21)

The gods and goddesses to whom the pagans offer sacrifice are not really God; an idol is nothing when compared to God. Yet this does not mean that they do not exist at all. On the contrary they do exist; they are demons, and those who worship them are enslaved to them.

Paul, like other Jews and Christians of his time, was convinced of the existence of these demonic powers and of their destructive influence on the lives of human beings. That viewpoint seems foreign to many, perhaps most, modern Christians. We tend to see the evil in the world as a result of the evil decisions that we as human beings make. We do not see the necessity of positing extra-human beings in order to explain the existence of evil in the world.

Yet even we experience evil as a massive reality which seems to go beyond the realm of the purely human, or at least which escapes satisfactory explanation at a purely human level. One need think only of the massive destruction of the Jews during Nazi rule in Europe. Yet the reality of evil as something beyond the control of individual human beings comes even closer to us in the inevitable fact of death. We all must die; yet death is not something that any of us choose nor is it something that, for the most part, anyone chooses on our behalf. We experience death as a kind of power over which we ultimately have no control, to which we are forced to submit, to which we are in a sense enslaved.

That experience of death comes very close to what Paul must have understood as the power of these demonic creatures who controlled human lives apart from God. In fact, Paul himself seems to have looked on death as a reality very similar to and even more destructive than that of the elemental spirits. In Romans 7:7-13 he describes sin and death as almost independent realities that work their will on human beings. They make use of the Mosaic Law, which in itself is good, to force themselves on human beings. These human beings are unwilling to submit, yet they are unable to resist the power of sin and death. It is perhaps at this point that our own contemporary experience of evil as a reality beyond human control comes closest to Paul's description of death and of the "weak and beggarly elemental spirits" of the universe.

Paul, then, sees God as a realm of power which overcomes those other, alien powers which seek to enslave and then destroy human existence. That realm of power is most clearly manifested in the crucifixion and resurrection of Jesus and will be completed in Jesus' coming in power; in that coming all things will be subjected to Jesus and Jesus will then subject all things to the Father (1 Cor 15:20-28).

While many of the elements that go into this viewpoint are to be found in either the Judaism of the period or the Christian traditions on which Paul drew, the way in which Paul used them and the emphasis that he gave to them was his own. All of these elements were refracted through the prism of his own personality and his own experience.

Real Power and Weakness

Yet it is not as if Paul's understanding of God and Jesus as a realm of power was simply Paul's own personality written large. Paul's own view of himself and especially his own sense of power were radically transformed. This transformation can be seen most clearly in 2 Corinthians 11:16—12:13. In this passage Paul lashes out at his opponents and their claim that they are better apostles than he is, that he is in fact weak as an apostle. In order to defend himself, he draws on and interprets his own work as an apostle and his own experience of God.

Since his opponents have boasted of their accomplishments as apostles, Paul asks the Corinthian Christians sarcastically to give him leave to foolishly boast of his own accomplishments. Even if it is foolishness to boast of one's accomplishments, the Corinthan Christians should be used to such boasting from Paul's opponents (2 Cor 11:16-21).

Paul then lists in a highly rhetorical style his own accomplishments. He begins in 2 Corinthians 11:22 by boasting of his own ancestry. If they are Hebrews, so is he; if they are Israelites, so is he; if they are descendants of Abraham, so is he. He then goes on in 2 Corinthians 11:23-29 to list all of the things that he has endured as a servant of Christ. He points to his imprisonments, his beatings, the many dangers that he faced during his journeys, his hunger, his thirst, his shipwrecks. All of these things he has endured as part of the daily anxiety which he has had on behalf of the churches that he has founded.

Then, all of a sudden, there is a change of tone in 2 Corinthians 11:30-33:

> [30]If I must boast, I will boast of the things that show my weakness. [31]The God and Father of the Lord Jesus, he who is blessed for ever, knows that I do not lie. [32]At Damascus, the governor under King Aretas guarded the city of Damascus in order to seize me, [33]but I was let down in a basket through a window in the wall, and escaped his hands.

Here Paul points not to his strengths but to his weaknesses. He describes this almost comic and certainly humiliating episode in which he is lowered through the city wall in a basket in order to avoid arrest. This small but comic episode gives us a hint of the direction in which Paul is heading.

But it is not a direction in which Paul immediately moves. Rather he resumes a list of his own accomplishments. He describes a vision that he had fourteen years prior to writing this letter to the Corinthians (2 Cor 12:1-4). It is a vision that took place after the vision on the road to Damascus, probably around A.D. 42. In this vision Paul is taken up in Christ into the third heaven where he hears things that "man may not utter." He concludes, however, that "on behalf of this man I will boast, but on my own behalf I will not boast, except in my weaknesses" (2 Cor 12:5).

The conclusion of his description of his own religious experience then leads him to take up again the themes of power and weakness.

> ⁶Though if I wish to boast, I shall not be a fool, for I shall be speaking the truth. But I refrain from it, so that no one may think more of me than he sees in me or hears from me. ⁷And to keep me from being too elated by the abundance of revelations, a thorn was given me in the flesh, a messenger of Satan, to harass me, to keep me from being too elated. ⁸Three times I besought the Lord about this, that it should leave me; ⁹but he said to me, "My grace is sufficient for you, for my power is made perfect in weakness." I will all the more gladly boast of my weaknesses, that the power of Christ may rest upon me. ¹⁰For the sake of Christ, then, I am content with weaknesses, insults, hardships, persecutions, and calamities; for when I am weak, then I am strong. (2 Cor 12:6-10).

At the climax of his list of accomplishments, Paul paradoxically boasts not of his strengths but of his weaknesses and of

what God had told him about those weaknesses and their
value. Over the centuries scholars have wondered what Paul's
"thorn in the flesh" was. Diseases such as epilepsy or a chronic
eye infection have been suggested. As a matter of fact, we do
not know what that disease was. What we do know is that
Paul found it disabling and three times begged God to remove
it from him and was three times refused.

Whatever the problem was, Paul suffered from it but was
convinced that in his suffering God's strength was at work in
him. This conviction worked a profound transformation of his
own understanding of what real strength and weakness
involved. For a person who saw the world in terms of power
and who saw himself as a person of power, a person who
accomplished what he set out to do, this was a deep and
paradoxical transformation. What he once saw as strength, his
own strength, he now sees as weakness when compared to
what God was accomplishing in him. On the other hand,
what he once saw as weakness, symbolized especially in his
suffering from this debilitating disease, he now sees as real
strength because it allowed God to work in and through him
in new and unexpected ways. God's power had been made
perfect in his weakness.

As Paul saw it, this paradoxical transformation took place
almost in spite of himself. He certainly did not seek the
suffering that came with his disease. As a matter of fact, he
sought three times to have it removed. Paul's interpretation of
his own suffering indicates that he did not actively seek out
suffering. Quite the contrary, he sought to avoid it and to rid
himself of it. He was not a masochist. But his own experience
of unavoidable yet painful suffering allowed him to see even in

that suffering God's power at work in him, working in a way that would have been impossible otherwise.

Conclusion

One can see, then, that the metaphors of power and weakness always remained central to Paul's life and his experience of God and Christ. Yet the meaning of those metaphors is transformed through his own experience of suffering and weakness and of God's transforming power at work in him. God and Christ are not simply mirror images of Paul's sense of his own power. Rather God and Christ have transformed Paul's own understanding of himself. It is no longer he who is powerful but God who works in him. All that he has accomplished as a Christian missionary, all that he has endured during his travels are now seen by him, not as examples of his own power but of a power infinitely greater than his own which is at work in him, especially in his weakness. That physical weakness is a constant reminder to Paul of whose power is really at work, lest Paul forget and think that what he has accomplished, he has accomplished on his own.

Paul's own convictions were derived both from Judaism and from early Christianity but were given a new perspective when they were filtered through the lens of his own experience. That perspective affects the way in which Paul understands all of the other beliefs and practices of his new-found faith. It affects how he looks on the Mosaic Law. It affects his view of how Christians should live, his view of Christian ethics. It affects how he looks on the conduct of "weaker" brothers and sisters. Finally, it affects the way in which he looks on the final consummation of the world when God will be victorious over every principality and power, victorious even over death. As in every spirituality, Paul has been guided by the interaction of tradition and experience, by what he has learned from others about God and by what he himself has experienced of God.

4

FAITH AND THE MOSAIC LAW

One of the most fateful controversies in early Christian history revolved around the question of whether or not Christians were bound to observe the Mosaic Law. As we know, the Christian churches for the most part decided that Christians did not have to observe the Mosaic Law as such. In retrospect that decision may seem obvious to twentieth-century Christians. Yet, when looked at from the point of view of the Christians of the first century, that decision was anything but obvious. In fact, just the opposite must have seemed the case for early Christians. All of the first disciples of Jesus, to say nothing of Jesus himself, were Jewish. The first Christians saw in Jesus the awaited Messiah or Christ, promised to them, as they believed, in the Scriptures of Judaism. The Jewish Scriptures were their scriptures, and at the center of those Scriptures was the Mosaic Law. The first "Christians" saw themselves not only as ethnically Jewish but also as religiously Jewish. Given all of that, it must have seemed obvious to them that they had to observe the Mosaic Law.

Yet within two or three generations, by roughly A.D. 100, most Christians were both ethnically and religiously non-Jewish, ethnically because the majority were Gentile in origin and religiously because they no longer observed the Mosaic Law, but saw themselves as members of a distinct religion. At the center of the controversy that led to those fateful results stood the apostle Paul. By examining the role that Paul played in that controversy and the arguments that he used in favor of not observing the Mosaic Law as such, we learn a great deal about Paul himself and about what he saw as crucial to faith in Jesus as the Christ.

The Jerusalem Conference

The controversy about whether Christians were bound to observe the Mosaic Law came to a head in early Christianity in A.D. 48 at a conference of Christian leaders which took place in Jerusalem. This conference was provoked by the fact that early Christian missionaries were making converts to belief in Jesus among non-Jews. Stories of some of those early conversions are found in the Acts of the Apostles (8, 10, 13—14). Paul was among those who were making Gentile converts, and he was adamantly opposed to demanding that they be obligated to observe the Mosaic Law. The question, then, of whether or not Gentile converts to belief in Jesus had to observe the Mosaic Law became a burning issue. That was the issue faced at the conference in Jerusalem in A.D. 48.

We have two versions of that conference, one from Paul himself in his letter to the Galatians (2:1-10) and the other in the Acts of the Apostles (15:1-21). Once again, a comparison between Paul's account of the conference and the account given by Luke in the Acts of the Apostles throws light on Paul and his understanding of belief in Christ. Both Paul and Luke have different views about the decision made by the conference and the reasons for that decision. These differences enable us to clarify Paul's own view of the Mosaic Law and its relationship to belief in Christ.

According to Luke the controversy came to a head when some Jewish Christians came from Jerusalem down to Antioch where Paul and his co-worker at the time, Barnabas, were staying. These Jewish Christans claimed that unless Gentile Christians were circumcised, they could not be saved. In the wake of the dissension that followed, Paul and Barnabas were appointed by the church in Antioch to go up to Jerusalem to resolve the question.

Paul, Barnabas, and other Christians from Antioch then went up to Jerusalem to talk with the apostles and elders of the Jerusalem community. After a good deal of debate, Peter rose and addressed the assembly.

> 7Brethren, you know that in the early days God made choice among you, that by my mouth the Gentiles should hear the word of the gospel and believe. 8And God who knows the heart bore witness to them, giving them the Holy Spirit just as he did to us; 9and he made no distinction between us and them, but cleansed their hearts by faith. 10Now therefore why do we make trial of God by putting a yoke upon the neck of the disciples which neither our fathers nor we have been able to bear? 11But we believe that we shall be saved through the grace of the Lord Jesus, just as they will. (Acts 15:7-11)

Peter gave two reasons why he believed that Gentile Christians should not be obligated to observe the Mosaic Law. The first reason (Acts 15:7-9) was that the Holy Spirit had been given to the Gentile Christians in the same way that it had been given to Jewish Christians. God, in other words, did not make a distinction between the two groups of people. The second reason that Peter gave was that they should not impose on the Gentiles a burden which they, as Jewish Christians, and their Jewish ancestors were unable to bear. Behind this reason lay the notion that it was impossible to observe all the precepts of the Mosaic Law.

The decision of this conference, according to Luke, was that Gentile Christians should not be forced to observe the Mosaic Law, with the exception of certain regulations (e.g., abstinence from unchastity, food offered to idols, and meat not properly butchered) which were thought to apply to Gentiles even before the coming of Christ (Acts 15:19-20). This decision, although arrived at after some debate, was in Luke's mind a consensus decision approved of by the apostles, the elders, and indeed the whole church. (Acts 15:22)

Paul's own version of the conference is found in Galatians 2:1-10, and his version differs significantly from that of Luke's:

> [1]Then after fourteen years I went up again to Jerusalem with Barnabas, taking Titus along with me. [2]I went up by revelation; and I laid before them (but privately before those who were of repute) the gospel which I preach among the Gentiles, lest somehow I should be running or had run in vain. [3]But even Titus, who was with me, was not compelled to be circumcised, though he was a Greek. [4]But because of false brethren secretly brought in, who slipped in to spy out our freedom which we have in Christ Jesus, that they might bring us into bondage— [5]to them we did not yield submission even for a moment, that the truth of the gospel might be preserved for you. [6]And from those who were reputed to be something (what they were

makes no difference to me; God shows no partiality)—those, I
say, who were of repute added nothing to me; [7]but on the
contrary, when they saw that I had been entrusted with the
gospel to the uncircumcised, just as Peter had been entrusted
with the gospel to the circumcised, [8](for he who worked
through Peter for the mission to the circumcised worked
through me also for the Gentiles), [9]and when they perceived the
grace that was given to me, James and Cephas and John, who
were reputed to be pillars, gave to me and Barnabas the right
hand of fellowship, that we should go to the Gentiles, and they
to the circumcised; [10]only they would have us remember the
poor, which very thing I was eager to do.

In the first place, Paul seems to have known nothing of the
regulations about refraining from unchastity, etc., which Luke
claimed to have been part of the agreement. Secondly, the
reasons given by Paul for the decision differ from those given
in Acts. Paul certainly agreed that the Holy Spirit had been
given to the Gentile Christians in the same way that it had
been given to Jewish Christians (see Gal 3:1-5). He says
nothing, however, about the fact that the observance of the
Mosaic Law was an unbearable burden for Jewish Christians
to observe. Rather, Paul saw the demand to observe the Mosaic
Law as an attempt to destroy the freedom which Gentile
Christians had in Christ and to lead Christians back into
bondage of some sort (Gal 2:4). For Paul such a demand was
an attack on the truth of the gospel, an attack that he firmly
resisted (Gal 2:5).

Paul Versus Luke

At first it may seem that there is little or no difference between Luke's notion that the Mosaic Law was an unbearable burden and Paul's that the observance of the Mosaic Law was a form of "bondage" for Christians. Yet, the rather cryptic reference in this section of the letter to the Galatians to the Mosaic Law as a form of bondage is clarified by other passages in Galatians, and that clarification reveals the extent to which Paul's concept of the value and function of the Mosaic Law differed from that of Luke.

At the beginning of his final exhortation to the Galatians, Paul once again takes up the metaphors of freedom and bondage (Gal 5:1-6):

> [1]For freedom Christ has set us free; stand fast therefore, and do not submit again to a yoke of slavery. [2]Now I, Paul, say to you that if you receive circumcision, Christ will be of no advantage to you. [3]I testify again to every man who receives circumcision that he is bound to keep the whole law. [4]You are severed from Christ, you who would be justified by the law; you have fallen away from grace .[5]For through the Spirit, by faith, we wait for the hope of righteousness. [6]For in Christ Jesus neither circumcision nor uncircumcision is of any avail, but faith working through love.

Here again we have the contrast of freedom versus slavery. But unlike the passage in Galatians 2, Paul clarifies what he means by that contrast. If you seek to be justified before God through the observance of the Mosaic Law, you are cut off from Christ. The reason for this is that for the Christian, justification comes by faith in Christ working through love, a faith experienced as the power of the Spirit in the life of the Christian. The central question for Paul was how one was to be justified. Was justification through the observance of the Mosaic Law, or was it through the experience of the Spirit by faith in Christ?

The Galatian Christians, perhaps urged on by Jewish-Christian missionaries from Jerusalem, were in danger of believing that justification was through *both* faith in Christ *and* observance of the Mosaic Law. For Paul, however, it could never be a question of both/and; it could only be a question of either/or. For him any attempt to place the observance of the Mosaic Law on the same level as faith in Christ meant, in the end, that faith in Christ was unnecessary for justification.

This aspect of Paul's position emerges most strongly in one of the most difficult passages of the Pauline letters, that is, in Galatians 2:11-21. This passage is an interpretation of an incident that took place in Antioch after the decision of the conference in Jerusalem. Peter had come to Antioch and was eating with the Gentiles. For a Pharisaic Jew such conduct inevitably meant that one was eating in a state of ritual impurity. It was incompatible with observance of the Mosaic Law. At first this did not seem to bother Peter. But then some Jewish Christians came to Antioch from Jerusalem. They were followers of James, perhaps the most prominent member of the Christian community in Jerusalem. At this point Peter stopped eating with the Gentile Christians and began to observe the demands of the Mosaic Law for ritual purity. At this point Paul opposed Peter and asked him: "If you, though a Jew, live like a Gentile and not like a Jew, how can you compel the Gentiles to live like Jews" (Gal 2:14)?

Using this incident as a starting point, Paul goes on to contrast observance of the Mosaic Law with justification by faith.

¹⁵We ourselves, who are Jews by birth and not Gentile sinners, ¹⁶yet who know that a man is not justified by works of the law but through faith in Jesus Christ, even we have believed in Christ Jesus, in order to be justified by faith in Christ, and not by works of the law, because by works of the law shall no one be justified. ¹⁷But if, in our endeavor to be justified in Christ, we ourselves were found to be sinners, is Christ then an agent of sin? Certainly not! ¹⁸But if I build up again those things which I tore down, then I prove myself a transgressor. ¹⁹For I through the law died to the law, that I might live to God. ²⁰I have been crucified with Christ; it is no longer I who live, but Christ who lives in me; and the life I now live in the flesh I live by faith in the Son of God, who loved me and gave himself for me. ²¹I do not nullify the grace of God; for if justification were through the law, then Christ died to no purpose. (Gal 2:15-21)

The line of argument of this passage is very compressed and difficult to follow. But if we look at the end of the passage (Gal 2:20-21), we get a clearer sense of what Paul was driving at and why he was so firm in his position. Since his call, Paul claims that it is no longer he who lives but Christ who lives in him. His own experience of Christ has become so central to him that he can talk of Christ as taking over his life and transforming it. This is the experiential side of his claim that he now lives by faith in the Son of God, that justification is by faith. To put any other claim beside that experience, even if that claim is for the observance of the Mosaic Law, is to nullify everything that Christ did, especially the fact of his death. In other words, Paul's own experience of Christ was so powerful that he could imagine no other religious act or observance that could be comparable to it. Even observance of the Mosaic Law paled in the face of that experience. To go back to the metaphor of freedom and slavery (Gal 2:4; 5:1), everything else was slavery, bondage, in comparison with the freedom that Paul experienced in Christ.

Paul took this position based not only on his own experience but also, he claimed, based on the experience of the Galatian Christians to whom he was writing.

> [1]O foolish Galatians! Who has bewitched you, before whose eyes Jesus Christ was publicly portrayed as crucified? [2]Let me ask you only this: Did you receive the Spirit by works of the law, or by hearing with faith? [3]Are you so foolish? Having begun with the Spirit, are you now ending with the flesh? [4]Did you experience so many things in vain?—if it really is in vain. [5]Does he who supplies the Spirit to you and works miracles among you do so by works of the law, or by hearing with faith? (Gal 3:1-5)

Paul asks the Galatian Christians to look to their own experience, to see whether his position tallies with their experience. He is asking them as Gentile Christians, who originally became Christians without the observance of the Mosaic Law, how they first experienced the transforming presence of the Spirit. The experience of the Spirit is another way Paul uses to talk about the kind of experience that he had at his call. Did that transforming experience of the Spirit happen to them by observing the Mosaic Law, or did it happen to them through faith in Christ? The obvious answer was that it happened through faith in Christ, since their fascination with the Mosaic Law came only later.

With all of this in mind, Paul's position on the relationship of faith in Christ to the observance of the Mosaic Law becomes clearer. In addition, it also becomes clearer how Paul's understanding of the Mosaic Law differs from Luke's. For Paul nothing, including the observance of the Mosaic Law, could be compared to or put on the same level with his or other Christians' transforming experience of the Spirit that came through faith in Christ. In that sense, everything else seemed like slavery and bondage when compared with the freedom that he experienced in the Spirit through faith.

This is very different from seeing the Mosaic Law as a burden that was impossible to observe, the viewpoint taken by Luke in Acts 15:10. On the contrary, Paul claims that prior to his call, his own observance of the Mosaic Law was faultless (Phil 3:5-6). He did not see the Mosaic Law as a jumble of legalistic regulations which was an impossible burden for people to bear. Rather the Mosaic Law paled into insignificance when compared with his own experience of Christ through faith.

Paul and the Mosaic Law

This insight goes a long way in explaining Paul's attitude toward the observance of the Mosaic Law. His understanding and evaluation of it is from a perspective, and that perspective is rooted in his overpowering and transforming experience of Christ through faith. Looked at from that perspective, the observance of the Mosaic Law as such was for Paul no longer necessary.

Throughout this chapter I have been careful to specify that our discussion has been about the contrast between faith in Christ and observance of the *Mosaic Law*. The reason for this emphasis is that, especially in the light of the debates between Catholics and Lutherans since the time of the Reformation, there is a tendency to think of the contrast as one between faith and *works*. The contrast becomes one between salvation through an absolute trust in the graciousness of God versus salvation through human achievement, that is, by works. "Observance of the law" became a catchword for salvation through human achievement. That way of putting the contrast says something about the way in which Christians of the sixteenth century and we twentieth-century Western Christians understand our own experiences. Yet it is to impose our way of experiencing and thinking about the world when we try to claim that that was what Paul was also saying in the first century. When Paul thought of law, he was thinking quite specifically about the Mosaic Law. He was not making statements primarily about law in general or about human experience in general for that matter. What he was claiming was that in the light of Christians' experience of Christ and his Spirit through faith, Christians were no longer bound by the observance of the Mosaic Law as such.

Yet Paul, as a Jew, could not simply dismiss the Mosaic Law so easily. He himself admitted to being a zealous observer of the Law prior to his call. Because of this he sought to justify his position not only through his own experience but also through his interpretation of the Scriptures. At first this may seem paradoxical, that Paul, who has just rejected the observance of the Mosaic Law, now tries to justify that rejection by appeal to the Scriptures whose center was that same Mosaic Law. But what Paul will claim is that it is the Scriptures themselves that point to a time when the necessity for observing the Mosaic Law as such will come to an end. Paul spends a good deal of time in both his letter to the Galatians and his letter to the Romans arguing from Scripture that in Christ that observance of the Mosaic Law has come to an end.

These arguments, which we shall look at in a moment, enlighten us about several crucial elements in Paul's religious outlook. In the first place, Paul's arguments from Scripture emphasize the extent to which he saw his faith in Christ as a fulfillment of his commitment to the God of Judaism. He felt the need to justify his commitment to Christ through an interpretation of those Scriptures which he believed were revealed by that same God. Secondly, it gives us an insight into the way in which Paul held experience and tradition in creative tension. Paul would not and indeed could not deny his or other Christians' experience of Christ. At the same time, however, he felt accountable to the tradition of Judaism. He felt that he had to make sense of his own experience within the context of that tradition, within the context of that tradition's Scriptures. Each threw light on the other, but neither could be set aside. He felt that he had to be true both to his experience and to his tradition.

Let us look at several examples of how he interpreted the Scriptures in the light of his own experience and how the Scriptures in turn threw light on his own experience. Both of these examples center around the figure of Abraham; one example is taken from Galatians (3:6-18), the other from Romans (4:1-25).

The first example is Paul's interpretation of God's promise to Abraham (Gen 15:1-6). This is a rather involved interpretation of the relationship of faith, the Mosaic Law, and the Gentiles. He begins by giving his interpretation of the story in Genesis 15, in which the Lord comes to Abraham in a vision and promises him that he will have a son and heir and that his descendants will be numberless. Abraham believed the Lord and this was reckoned to him as righteousness (Gen 15:6).

Paul begins his interpretation with Genesis 15:6:

> ⁶Thus Abraham "believed God, and it was reckoned to him as
> righteousness." ⁷So you see that it is men of faith who are the
> sons of Abraham. ⁸And the scripture, foreseeing that God would
> justify the Gentiles by faith, preached the gospel beforehand to
> Abraham, saying, "In you shall all the nations be blessed" (Gen
> 12:3; 18:18). ⁹So then, those who are men of faith are blessed
> with Abraham who had faith. (Gal 3:6-9)

In this passage, Paul tries to bring together what he thinks are
crucial elements in the Abraham story. In the first place, it was
Abraham's belief or faith in God that made Abraham just or
righteous in God's eyes. Secondly, the real descendants of
Abraham are those who, like Abraham, have faith. Thirdly,
Paul emphasizes the importance of a particular aspect of the
blessing given to Abraham, that is, that through Abraham all
the nations would be blessed. The same word (*goiim* in
Hebrew, *ethnē* in Greek) means both "nations" and "Gentiles."
Paul's interpretation of this blessing was that through Abraham's faith the Gentiles would eventually be blessed. Put
another way, those who are descendants of Abraham through
a faith like Abraham's would be blessed; and among those
descendants of Abraham by faith would be the Gentiles.

Paul then goes on to argue that it is through Christ that this
blessing given to Abraham comes to the Gentiles (Gal 3:14).
One of the reasons that Paul will argue that it is through
Christ that these blessings come to the Gentiles is that the
promises were made to Abraham and to his offspring (Gen
12:7; 13:5; 17:7; 22:18). Since the word "offspring" is in the
singular and not the plural, Paul argues that it must refer to
one person and not to many. That one person, of course, is
Christ; and so it is through Christ that the promises made to

Abraham, the promises given because of Abraham's faith, come to the Gentiles.

From the point of view of modern critical interpretation of the Old Testament, Paul's interpretation seems strained. After all, the term "offspring" that Paul interprets as referring to Christ in the text of Genesis is a collective noun and so refers to the whole people. Paul himself will take it in that sense in Romans 4:16-18. Yet Paul was using methods of interpretation which were common in the first century A.D. to make his case. He was interpreting the religious texts of Judaism to make the case that those texts themselves pointed to the figure of Christ and to a time when the blessing of Abraham would come to the Gentiles through the same kind of faith that Abraham had.

The second example comes from the letter to the Romans. Once again, Paul returns to an interpretation of the figure of Abraham (Rom 4:1-25). In the interpretation given in Romans, it becomes clearer why Abraham was so attractive to Paul.

> [9]Is this blessing pronounced only upon the circumcised, or also upon the uncircumcised? We say that faith was reckoned to Abraham as righteousness. [10]How then was it reckoned to him? Was it before or after he had been circumcised? It was not after, but before he was circumcised. [11]He received circumcision as a sign or seal of the righteousness which he had by faith while he was still uncircumcised. The purpose was to make him father of all who believe without being circumcised and who thus have righteousness reckoned to them, [12]and likewise the father of the circumcised who are not merely circumcised but also follow the example of the faith which our father Abraham had before he was circumcised. (Rom 4:9-12)

Paul's argument is that Abraham's faith and the righteousness which was given to him because of that faith (Gen 15:6) came to him *before* he was circumcised (Gen 17:9-14, 22-27). Because of that the blessings given to Abraham were given not only to Jews but also were meant for Gentiles. Once again, modern critical interpretation of Genesis would find Paul's argument forced. Yet he was giving a close, detailed interpretation of the Genesis text based on principles of interpretation which were in keeping with the critical principles of his own day.

From the way in which Paul interprets the story of Abraham, one can begin to see why the figure of Abraham was so fascinating and so important to Paul. Abraham represented almost a mirror image of the position in which Paul saw himself and other early Christians. Abraham's righteousness, like their own, was due to his faith and trust in God and not to his observance of the Mosaic Law. In addition, Abraham, at least as Paul interpreted him, was a figure who was prior to the split between Jew and Gentile. In Paul's mind, Abraham's faith came into existence prior to the division between Jew and Gentile, which occurred at Abraham's circumcision, just as his own faith and that of other early Christians existed after the gap between Jew and Gentile had been bridged in the figure of Jesus.

What emerges most clearly from these two examples is the importance which Paul gives to the Scriptures and their interpretation. It was important for Paul that his own experience of Christ be in continuity with what had been revealed by God in the Scriptures. Those Scriptures, however, were not some general "revealed scriptures" but quite specifically the Scriptures of Judaism. Paul, then, saw his own experience of

Christ as something that was in continuity with Judaism and with Judaism's God.

For Paul it was the Jewish Scriptures themselves which point to a time when it would no longer be necessary to observe the Mosaic Law which is contained in those Scriptures. As a consequence, both the Jewish Scriptures and the Mosaic Law contained in them were for Paul matters of revelation. The Mosaic Law was not a jumble of legalistic regulations which had been a burden for Jews both past and present to observe. Rather, the Mosaic Law was part of God's revelation. In this Paul was faithful to his own Jewish roots. What distinguished Paul from most of his fellow Jews, and from a number of his fellow believers in Jesus, was his conviction that the necessity for observing the Mosaic Law as such had come to an end through faith in Christ. For him faith in Christ and the power that comes as a result of that faith made possible a new way of life that no longer required the Mosaic Law.

What is also clear from his interpretations of the example of Abraham is that the end of the observance of the Mosaic Law made possible a new relationship between Jews and Gentiles. This is another major conclusion that he draws from his interpretation of the figure of Abraham in the letter to the Galatians:

> [27]For as many of you as were baptized into Christ have put on Christ. [28]There is neither Jew nor Greek, there is neither slave nor free, there is neither male nor female; for you are all one in Christ Jesus. [29]And if you are Christ's, then you are Abraham's offspring, heirs according to promise. (Gal 3:27-29)

The division, then, between Jew and Gentile is abolished through faith in Christ and baptism into Christ. Those observances which are particular to Judaism, specifically the Mosaic Law, and which consequently distinguished Jew from Gentile, are at an end.

Conclusion

Paul's position, then, on that crucial question within early Christianity, on the observance of the Mosaic Law, also reveals some of Paul's own central convictions and concerns. It reveals, first of all, the central role that his own religious experience and that of other early Christians played in his religious viewpoint. His experience of Christ was the vantage point from which he saw everything else. That experience was so central and so overpowering that no other experience, even that of observing the Mosaic Law, could be placed parallel with it. In the light of that experience all else faded into insignificance, including the Mosaic Law. It is quite clear from Paul's interpretation of the figure of Abraham that it was his own experience of faith in Christ that made possible an interpretation of the story of Abraham which made Abraham's faith the central element in that story.

Secondly, while Paul's religious experience was central, it was not to be accepted uncritically. He felt called upon to examine the Jewish Scriptures to see whether that experience was in some way compatible with those Scriptures. The effort that he expended in the interpretation of those Scriptures makes clear that such an examination was no schoolbook exercise for him. He could not allow or even imagine that his and his fellow early Christians' experience was at odds with the revealed Scriptures of Judaism. This meant that Paul neither could nor would be unfaithful to his own Jewish roots, to his own Jewish tradition. While most of his fellow Jews, then and now, would evaluate his interpretations of the Jewish Scriptures very differently, Paul certainly intended to be faithful to Judaism and Judaism's God. This is crucial to remember, if only because Paul sometimes has been viewed mistakenly in Christian tradition as someone who condemned the Mosaic Law as a set of narrow, legalistic regulations.

Finally, one sees in Paul's convictions about the place of the Mosaic Law his concern that in Christ the basic division between human beings, the division between Jew and Gentile, has been abolished through faith in Christ. This reflects Paul's own conviction of the universal possibility of the experience of the power of God in Christ. As we shall see, that conviction will finally include not only the Gentiles but also his fellow Jews.

5

ETHICAL PERSPECTIVES:
THE SPIRIT AND SIN

The angriest letter Paul ever wrote was the one he wrote to the Christian communities in Galatia. He was so angry that he did not even include a thanksgiving at the beginning of the letter, a thanksgiving that is found at the beginning of all of Paul's other letters. As we saw earlier, Jewish-Christian missionaries from Jerusalem came to Galatia and began to preach that Christians must not only believe in Jesus but also that they were obligated to observe the Mosaic Law. Paul adamantly opposed them for two reasons. First, because his own religious experience of faith in Christ was so powerful, he refused to have anything else, including the Mosaic Law, placed on an equal footing with that experience. Salvation was through faith in Christ, not through the observance of the Mosaic Law. Second, because he was convinced that this experience of Christ was offered to all men and women, the distinction between Jew and Gentile had been abolished and with it the necessity of observing the Mosaic Law.

Yet if this observance was no longer required of them, how did Christians know how to act, what to do and what not to do? What became of ethics or ethical actions? If the observance of the Mosaic Law was no longer required of Christians, what ethical guidelines were valid, or were Christians exempt from ethical requirements altogether?

These kinds of questions were undoubtedly the kinds of questions that were put to Paul because of his position on the relationship of faith in Christ to the observance of the Mosaic Law. Perhaps the best way to understand how Paul dealt with these problems is to examine more closely the reasons for the Galatian Christians' fascination with the Mosaic Law and then to contrast that fascination with Paul's own ethical perspectives.

Fascination with the Mosaic Law

Why were the Galatians fascinated with the Mosaic Law? Why were they so attracted by the notion that, in addition to faith in Christ, Christians should observe it? One must try to imagine how the Galatians must have experienced their conversion to faith in Christ. The Christian communities of Galatia were predominantly, perhaps exclusively, converts to Christian faith from various Graeco-Roman religious cults. They were not ethnically Jewish. With groups such as the Galatian Christians we can talk of real "conversions." They changed from one religion to another. To be more specific, their conversion to Christian faith meant the simultaneous rejection of the various religious traditions to which they had belonged, including the various civic religions of the cities and towns in which they lived and worked. It meant turning their backs on the religious beliefs of their fellow citizens and, in many cases, on the religious beliefs of their own families.

In the ancient world, this kind of religious conversion was restricted primarily to converts to Judaism and, following Judaism, to faith in Jesus. In most of the religious cults of the Graeco-Roman world, conversion was not at all an important concept. If one adhered to one religious cult, it did not mean that one could not also practice some other cult. Often one participated in several cults at the same time. One participated in the cults of the city or town in which one lived; one participated in civic religion. At the same time, one participated in the cults that were part of one's own family or ethnic group, in the cult of the profession to which one belonged, or in a mystery cult to which one belonged of one's own free will as an individual. To practice one cult in no way excluded participation in other cults.

In this respect Judaism, and then Christianity following Judaism, stood apart from the normal practice of the Graeco-Roman world. To become a Jew or a Christian meant that one turned one's back on the practices of all other religious cults. In his letter to the Galatians, Paul refers to the religious practices of the Galatians prior to their conversion as a "bondage to beings that by nature are no gods" (Gal 4:8). In 1 Thessalonians Paul describes how the Thessalonians, another group of Gentile converts, "turned to God from idols, to serve a living and true God, and to wait for his Son from heaven, whom he raised from the dead, Jesus, who delivers us from the wrath to come" (1 Thess 1:9-10). To become a Christian meant not only turning to something, faith in Christ; it also meant turning away from the worship of all gods and goddesses.

One has to imagine, then, how difficult a conversion of this sort must have been for people living in the Graeco-Roman world. It meant the rejection of the whole fabric of religious practices that were part of the warp and woof of life in an ancient city or town. It meant the rejection of all that one's fellow citizens and family held dear, of all that both city and family thought were at the basis of the continued prosperity of the city and the family. To be a convert of this sort meant that one not only rejected this or that religious practice but that one also opted out of central elements of the civic life of the world in which one lived. One was not only a "convert," one was in a sense a traitor. From this perspective one can understand why both Jews and Christians were sometimes thought of as atheists and subversives.

Within this context one can begin to see why the Galatian Christians might have been so attracted to the observance of the Mosaic Law. One must remember that it was not simply and not primarily a set of commands and prohibitions. It was a way of life. It gave structure and religious meaning to the various activities of one's daily life. It was a way of worshipping God and a way of establishing and maintaining one's religious identity in relationship to that God. Once the Galatian Christians had rejected the religious structures and practices of their fellow countrymen, the observance of the Mosaic Law offered them the possibility of establishing a new religious identity and a new structure for their lives. In this sense, it offered them a new framework for determining what to do and what not to do.

The Spirit and the Flesh

Paul, however, saw things differently. He felt that the demand that Christians observe the Mosaic Law placed the Mosaic Law on the same level as faith in Christ. In the light of his own experience, that was impossible. In addition, he felt that the demand that Christians observe the Mosaic Law also preserved the distinction between Jew and Gentile, a distinction that Paul felt had been abolished through faith in Christ.

But Paul's objection to Christians observing the Mosaic Law also had to do with his own sense of what the central ethical dilemma of human life really was. For the Galatian Christians, that dilemma concerned the problem of *what* to do and *what* not to do. For Paul, however, the central ethical question was not really a matter of *what* but a matter of *how*. As one reads the ethical sections of his letters, Paul is not in doubt about what one was to do or not to do. The *what* of ethics was not for Paul the primary ethical question. Rather, he was primarily concerned with the question of *how* one was able to do what one knew was right and *how* one avoided doing what one knew was wrong. It was a question of power rather than a question of knowledge.

For Paul this new power that was present in the lives of Christians was the power of the Spirit at work in them. This becomes clear as Paul writes to the Galatian Christians about how they are to live their Christian lives.

> [16]But I say, walk by the Spirit, and do not gratify the desires of the flesh. [17]For the desires of the flesh are against the Spirit, and the desires of the Spirit are against the flesh; for these are opposed to each other, to prevent you from doing what you

would. ¹⁸For if you are led by the Spirit you are not under the
law. (Gal 5:16-18)

Paul begins by contrasting the Spirit with the desires of the
flesh. The two are at odds with one another. In this context it is
as important to understand what Paul is not talking about as
much as it is to understand what he is talking about. The
contrast between the Spirit and the flesh is not between soul
and body. The Spirit in the passage as well as in the rest of
Paul's letters is primarily God's power at work in the lives of
Christians. Earlier in Galatians Paul appeals to their own
experience of that Spirit, of that divine power at work in their
lives (Gal 3:1-5). The Spirit, then, is not the human soul in
contrast to the human body.

Similarly, the "flesh" is not for Paul to be identified with
the human body. Later in Galatians Paul lists a series of vices
which he characterizes as "works of the flesh":

> ¹⁹Now the works of the flesh are plain: fornication, impurity,
> licentiousness, ²⁰idolatry, sorcery, enmity, strife, jealousy, anger,
> selfishness, dissension, party spirit, ²¹envy, drunkenness, carous-
> ing, and the like. (Gal 5:19-21)

The majority of the vices that Paul lists (idolatry, sorcery,
enmity, strife, jealousy, anger, selfishness, dissension, party
spirit, and envy) are not vices that one usually associates with
the body. They are, rather, vices of the human soul, "spiritual"
vices, if you will. What Paul means by the "flesh" is not the
human body but that element of the whole human person
which draws the person away from the love of God and love of
neighbor. It is whatever in us resists the power of the Spirit.

Paul takes up this same contrast between the Spirit and the

flesh and expands on it in Romans 8. In Romans 8:1-30 Paul develops the theme that "the law of the Spirit of life in Christ Jesus has set me free from the law of sin and death" (Rom 8:2). This section of Romans is divided into three parts:

8:1-13: Christian life as empowered by the Spirit

8:14-17: Adoptive children and the Spirit

8:18-30: Possession of the Spirit as the hope of glory

In the first of these three sections (Rom 8:1-13) Paul once again uses the contrast of Spirit and flesh. To set one's mind on the flesh is death while to set one's mind on the Spirit is life and peace. Those who live according to the flesh set their minds on the things of the flesh, while those who live according to the Spirit set their minds on the things of the Spirit. Once again, one has the same kind of contrast that one had in the letter to the Galatians.

But Paul also talks in more detail about the identity and function of this Spirit. It is first of all the Spirit of life in Christ Jesus (Rom 8:2). The experience of that Spirit is made possible through the sending of God's Son in the likeness of sinful flesh and for sin. The power of the Spirit for Paul is released through the death and resurrection of Jesus. In Romans 8:9-10 Paul speaks of the indwelling of the Spirit and the Spirit of Christ in parallel formulations. He also speaks of this Spirit as the Spirit of God (Rom 8:9) and the Spirit "of him who raised Jesus from the dead" (Rom 8:11). The Spirit, then, is also the Spirit of God the Father. Finally, he speaks of this Spirit as a power which dwells in the Christian which makes it possible for the Christian not to be in the flesh and so to belong to Christ (Rom 8:9).

What Paul is emphasizing in these descriptions is that through the death and resurrection of Jesus, a divine power is present in the lives of Christians, a divine power that is altogether new and different. This becomes more apparent in Romans 8:2-3:

> [2]For the law of the Spirit of life in Christ Jesus has set me free from the law of sin and death. [3]For God has done what the law, weakened by the flesh, could not do.

In these two short verses, Paul is summing up a good deal of what he has said in much more detail in Romans 6-7. His point is that the power of the Spirit in the lives of Christians can accomplish in them something new, something that the Mosaic Law could not accomplish. While the Mosaic Law was good and holy (Rom 7:12), it nevertheless could not stem the tide of sin and death because of human weakness brought about by the power of the flesh. It is rather the power of the Spirit that can overcome the drag of the flesh, the drag of everything that turns one away from God.

The second section (Rom 8:14-17) introduces a new metaphor to explain the reality of the Spirit in the lives of Christians:

> [14]For all who are led by the Spirit of God are sons of God. [15]For you did not receive the spirit of slavery to fall back into fear, but you have received the spirit of sonship. When we cry, "Abba, Father!" [16]it is the Spirit himself bearing witness with our spirit that we are children of God, [17]and if children, then heirs, heirs of God and fellow heirs with Christ, provided we suffer with him that we may also be glorified with him.

Another way of talking of the effects of the presence of the Spirit is to talk of Christians as children of God, and looking to the future, as heirs with Christ of the kingdom of God. This future inheritance, however, is conditioned by the notion that

Christians must also suffer with Christ.

The third section (Rom 8:18-30) expands on the notion of suffering and the relationship of suffering to the future. For Paul the sufferings of the present time are not even worthy to be compared with the glory that is to be revealed in the future (Rom 8:18). For Paul all of creation and human beings along with creation are eagerly awaiting the final consummation of the world. In this interim period it is the Spirit that teaches Christians how to pray, how to properly live and endure suffering in this interim period (Rom 8:26-27).

The Spirit then is a divine power which is present in the lives of Christians. The experience of that divine power serves as the basis for how Paul views the way Christians are to live their lives. The crucial ethical dilemma for Paul then was not what one was to do but how, by what power, one was enabled to do it.

The Fruits of the Spirit

This same ethical perspective emerges when one looks at the ways in which Paul describes the results of this experience of the Spirit. When one looks at these results, one also gets a more detailed sense of what he means when he talks about this experience.

One way in which he talks about the results of the experience of the Spirit is by listing virtues which he describes as the "fruit of the Spirit."

[22]But the fruit of the spirit is love, joy, peace, patience, kindness, goodness, faithfulness, [23]gentleness, self-control; against such there is no law. [24]And those who belong to Christ Jesus have

crucified the flesh with its passions and desires. [25]If we live by the Spirit, let us also walk by the Spirit. [26]Let us have no self-conceit, no provoking of one another, no envy of one another. (Gal 5:22-26)

When Paul speaks of the results of the power of the Spirit, he does not list a series of commands or prohibitions but rather a list of virtues. As one looks at this list of virtues, they are virtues which, for the most part, would have been praised both by his Graeco-Roman contemporaries and by his fellow Jews. In other words, the virtues were not exclusively Christian in themselves. Rather, Paul thought that it was through the power of the Spirit that Christians were able to practice those virtues that everyone felt were truly virtues. Once again, it was not the contents of ethical reflections which were Paul's primary concern but the question of the power by which one was able to put those virtues into practice.

In this passage from Galatians, Paul also makes a short but revealing remark about the relationship between the fruit of the Spirit and the law. In Galatians 5:23 Paul comments that there is no "law" against the practice of these virtues. Paul claims that those who belong to Christ, have crucified the flesh with its passions and desires, and who practice these virtues, are no longer in the realm of law. Through the practice of these virtues by the power of the Spirit, the Mosaic Law and the observance of its prohibitions and commands is a thing of the past. The point, of course, is not that Christians can now do whatever they want but that through the power of the Spirit they will do those things which were once a matter of command and prohibition in the Mosaic Law. Christians do not live by a different standard of conduct so much as they live by a new and different power.

A second way in which Paul describes the results of the experience of the Spirit is by describing the kinds of activities or functions which come from this experience. The most elaborate description of this sort is found in 1 Corinthians 12-14, a description and explanation of the "spiritual gifts." The specific question that Paul deals with in this section of 1 Corinthians concerns the practice of speaking in tongues, a kind of ecstatic prayer in the power of the Spirit. He wants to put that kind of prayer, that specific gift of the Spirit, in perspective. For Paul the gifts of the Spirit are to be evaluated in terms of their relationship to the common good of the Christian community.

> ⁴Now there are varieties of gifts; but the same Spirit; ⁵and there are varieties of service, but the same Lord; ⁶and there are varieties of working, but it is the same God who inspires them all in every one. ⁷To each is given the manifestation of the Spirit for the common good. (1 Cor 12:4-7)

Paul then lists a number of functions in the Christian community which are inspired by the Holy Spirit: the utterance of wisdom, the utterance of knowledge, faith, gifts of healing, working of miracles, prophecy, the discernment of spirits, speaking in tongues, and the interpretation of tongues. According to Paul all of these functions are inspired by one and the same Spirit. Later in the same chapter, he offers a different list: apostles, prophets, teachers, workers of miracles, healers, helpers, administrators, and speakers in various kinds of tongues (1 Cor 12:27-30). In this latter list Paul explicitly mentions that he is listing these functions in their order of importance (1 Cor 12:28). The reason that he lists them in this order is that the higher gifts are of more importance for the common good of the Christian community (see 1 Cor 12:7). A crucial element in Paul's ethical perspective, then, is his conviction about the centrality of the common good, of the Christian community itself. All of these gifts which come from the Spirit are meant for the good of the community and not simply for the development of the individual.

Views of Human Sinfulness

Paul's ethical perspective is dominated by the experience of the Spirit that is possessed by Christians, a divine power present in the lives of Christians which enables them to live in a new way. After one understands that perspective, one can then go on to ask a further question. How did Paul think of ethics and the ethical life prior to or apart from the experience of the Spirit? If it is the Spirit that empowers Christians to live as they are called to live, can those who do not experience the Spirit live as they should? If they cannot live as they should, are they culpable for not living that way, especially since they have not received the power of the Spirit? Paul's answers to those questions are not altogether consistent. At times he writes as if those who do not possess the Spirit are culpable for doing those things which they know to be wrong. At other times, however, Paul seems to claim that without the power of the Spirit a person is simply unable to do what he or she knows to be right. In that case, the person could not be held responsible for not doing what he or she was incapable of doing in the first place.

Perhaps the best way to illustrate this inconsistency is to look at two passages from his letter to the Romans. The first part of Romans (1:16—3:31) deals with the relationship between justification by faith and human sinfulness. Paul's thesis is stated in Romans 1:16-17:

> [16]For I am not ashamed of the gospel: it is the power of God for salvation to every one who has faith, to the Jew first and also to the Greek. [17]For in it the righteousness of God is revealed through faith for faith; as it is written, "The righteous shall live by faith."

This is, of course, one of Paul's fundamental convictions, that justification comes through faith in Christ, a faith which is the power of God in the life of the Christian.

Paul then contrasts this justification through faith in Christ with human sinfulness (Rom 1:18—3:20). He first describes the sinful situation of the Gentiles (Rom 1:18-32). The fundamental sin of the Gentiles is idolatry. For Paul, and for Jews of that period in general, God could be known from creation. The invisible nature of God could be perceived through those things God had made. The sin of the Gentiles was that, while they could have known God from creation, they chose not to honor God as God. Rather they chose to exchange "the glory of the immortal God for images resembling mortal man or birds or animals or reptiles" (Rom 1:23). In this choice, they were without excuse; they were responsible for their actions. As a result of this choice, God gave them up to all sorts of immorality. The immoral practices of the Gentiles, according to Paul, were punishments imposed on them by God for their more fundamental sin of idolatry.

Paul then turns his attention from the sinfulness of the Gentiles to that of the Jews. The Jews, of course, were not guilty of the sin of idolatry; they worshiped the true God. For

Paul, however, they were nevertheless sinful. Their sinfulness consisted in their failure to observe the Mosaic Law, a gift given to them by God.

> [17]But if you call yourself a Jew and rely upon the law and boast of your relation to God [18]and know his will and approve what is excellent, because you are instructed in the law, [19]and if you are sure that you are a guide to the blind, a light to those who are in darkness, [20]a corrector of the foolish, a teacher of children, having in the law the embodiment of knowledge and truth— [21]you then who teach others, will you not teach yourself? While you preach against stealing, do you steal? [22]You who say that one must not commit adultery, do you commit adultery? You who abhor idols, do you rob temples? [23]You who boast in the law, do you dishonor God by breaking the law? [24]For, as it is written, "The name of God is blasphemed among the Gentiles because of you." (Rom 2:17-24)

The conclusion that Paul draws from all of this is that both Jews and Gentiles are sinners. They are sinners for very different reasons, the Gentiles for idolatry and the Jews for breaking the Law; nevertheless both groups are sinners. Paul states this most clearly in Romans 3:9: "What then? Are we Jews any better off? No, not at all; for I have already charged that all men, both Jews and Greeks, are under the power of sin."

While it may not be immediately apparent, Paul has taken two very traditional types of Jewish literature and combined them in such a way as to come to a new conclusion. He has combined the traditional Jewish polemic against the Gentiles' idolatry with the equally traditional prophetic polemic against Jews who break the covenant between God and his people, and has drawn the novel conclusion that both Gentiles and

Jews stand *equally* under the judgment of God.

As one reads this twofold polemic, it seems quite clear that both Gentiles and Jews are responsible for their actions. They could have chosen to do otherwise, but by and large they did not. One would expect that Paul, following the polemic of the prophets, would hold both himself and his fellow Jews, responsible for their actions. But he also holds the Gentiles responsible for their actions. He points out that there are some Gentiles who by nature do what the Law requires. These Gentiles are a kind of "law" unto themselves. The law is written in their hearts (Rom 2:14-16). This means that the Gentiles were capable of doing what was right. The fact that a few did indicates just that possibility. But, for the most part, they chose not to do what they knew was right. Both Jews and Gentiles, then, were responsible for their own sinful actions.

When one turns to Romans 7, however, one gets a rather different evaluation of the relationship between human sinfulness and human responsibility for sin. Romans 7, among other things, is a qualified defense of the Mosaic Law and a description of the Christian's relationship to that Law. In Romans 7:1-6 Paul takes an analogy from marriage law. A married woman is bound to her husband as long as he lives. But as soon as her husband dies, she is free of the law concerning him. In a similar fashion, Christians have died to the obligation of observing the Mosaic Law through being joined to the body of Christ. Through his death, Christians have also died to the Mosaic Law. Paul concludes that "now we are discharged from the Law, dead to that which held us captive, so that we serve not under the old written code but in the new life of the Spirit" (Rom 7:6).

Given that view of the relationship of Christians to the

Mosaic Law, the obvious question was: Is the Law then sin? Paul spends the rest of the chapter defending the goodness and holiness of the Mosaic Law. In Romans 7:7-13 Paul argues that its role was to make known what sin was and what was sinful. In that sense the Law was holy and its commandments were holy and just and good (Rom 7:12). But, Paul argues, sin used the Law as an opportunity to deceive human beings and so bring about their deaths.

> [13]Did that which is good (i.e., the Law), then, bring death to me? By no means! It was sin, working death in me through what is good, in order that sin might be shown to be sin, and through the commandment might become sinful beyond measure. (Rom 7:13)

In this viewpoint, sin and sinfulness take on a reality quite different from the one found in Romans 1-3. In Romans 7, sin and death emerge as almost independent powers which dominate human existence, powers over which human beings have very little control.

This impression becomes even stronger when one reads the last section of this chapter (Rom 7:14-25). This section contains one of the more famous passages in Paul's letters.

> [14]We know that the Law is spiritual; but I am carnal, under sin. [15]I do not understand my own actions. For I do not do what I want, but I do the very thing I hate. [16]Now if I do what I do not want, I agree that the Law is good. [17]So then it is no longer I that do it, but sin which dwells within me. [18]For I know that nothing good dwells within me, that is, in my flesh. I can will what is right, but I cannot do it. [19]For I do not do the good I want, but the evil I do not want is what I do. [20]Now if I do what I do not want, it is no longer I that do it, but sin which dwells within me. (Rom 7:14-20)

This passage is one of the most difficult in Paul to interpret. It is also one of the most controversial. The arguments center around the identity of the "I" in this passage. Interpreters argue whether the passage gives a psychological analysis of the condition of human beings after the sin of Adam, the religious history of Paul before his conversion, the life of the Jews under the Mosaic Law, or perhaps the life of Adam. Given Paul's claim in Philippians 3:6 that he was blameless as to righteousness under the law, it seems unlikely that the "I" in this passage from Romans 7 refers to himself or to his own psychological state prior to his call. The "I" must stand for something more general; whether it is everyman, Adam, or the Jews under the law is less clear.

For our purposes, however, what is important is that human beings in this passage do not seem to have the power to control their own actions, either for good or for ill. In that sense, they can no longer be held responsible or culpable for their sinful actions. This is a rather different viewpoint than the one found in Romans 1—3. The question is whether, according to Paul, human beings are or are not responsible or culpable for their evil actions.

The answer is that Paul is not consistent in his responses to the problem of human responsibility. The reason for this seeming lack of consistency is that Paul perceived the question of human responsibility as a secondary or derivative question. What was central for Paul was the universal possibility of salvation in Christ. This becomes clearer when one notices what Paul does with his treatment of the problem of human responsibility and sinfulness in Romans 1—3 and Romans 7.

Before he began his description of human sinfulness in Romans 1:18—3:20, he set the problem in the context of salvation through faith in Christ:

> [16]For I am not ashamed of the gospel: it is the power of God for
> salvation to every one who has faith, to the Jew first and also to
> the Greek. [17]For in it the righteousness of God is revealed
> through faith for faith; as it is written, "He who is righteous shall
> live by faith." (Rom 1:16-17)

He then takes up that same theme again in Romans 3:21-24.

> [21]But now the righteousness of God has been manifested apart
> from law, although the law and the prophets bear witness to it,
> [22]the righteousness of God through faith in Jesus Christ for all
> who believe. For there is no distinction; [23]since all have sinned
> and fall short of the glory of God, [24]they are justified by his grace
> as a gift through the redemption which is in Christ Jesus.

Paul is describing human sinfulness from a certain perspective,
that is, from the perspective of salvation experienced through
faith in Christ. This experience of salvation in Christ is for
Paul something that is possible for all human beings, for both
Jews and Gentiles. It is from this perspective of the experience
of salvation through faith in Christ that Paul describes the
human condition apart from that experience. For Paul, both
Jews and Gentiles stand in need of that experience, the kind of
experience that transformed his own life and that of other
early Christians. In other words, Paul is not primarily inter-
ested in describing the sinful human condition in itself; rather,
he wants to contrast the experience of both Jews and Gentiles
without Christ with the overwhelming experience of life lived
through faith in Christ.

Paul is doing the same thing in Romans 8, the section of the
letter which follows his terrifying description of human powerlessness in Romans 7 and which we looked at earlier in this

chapter. After describing human wretchedness in Romans 7, he contrasts that wretchedness with the experience of the Spirit in Christ:

> [1]There is therefore now no condemnation for those who are in Christ Jesus. [2]For the law of the Spirit of life in Christ Jesus has set me free from the law of sin and death. [3]For God has done what the law, weakened by the flesh could not do: sending his own Son in the likeness of sinful flesh and for sin, he condemned sin in the flesh, [4]in order that the just requirement of the law might be fulfilled in us, who walk not according to the flesh but according to the Spirit. (Rom 8:1-4)

Once again, Paul is not trying to describe human powerlessness for its own sake. Rather, that description serves as a contrast to what has now been experienced through the Spirit of life in Christ Jesus.

Conclusion

What this means, then, is that Paul is describing human sinfulness and human powerlessness from the perspective of what he and other early Christians have experienced through faith in Christ. In comparison with that experience, human existence, apart from that experience seemed somehow fundamentally flawed and profoundly miserable. But what remained central was the experience itself. Paul was less concerned with the consistency of his description of human existence apart from the experience of faith in Christ than with highlighting the centrality of that experience by contrasting it with any human existence apart from it.

Paul's ethical perspectives, then, are part of the larger

pattern of his religious sensibilities. Ethical questions and ethical dilemmas are seen from the perspective of the experience of the empowerment of the Spirit through faith in Christ. That experience of empowerment enables the Christian to live in a new way, to act in a way that was previously impossible. Paul was less concerned with consistently describing that previous way of life than he was about showing how the situation was radically changed for the Christian through the experience of the Spirit in faith. Paul's was not primarily the troubled conscience finally delivered from agony through faith in Christ. Rather Paul's was the conscience radically changed and newly empowered in a way previously unimaginable.

6

ETHICS IN PRACTICE: FREEDOM AND COMMUNITY

Paul was no systematic theologian. His ethical perspectives were not altogether consistent, nor were his explanations of the human condition apart from Christ. Yet there was a fundamental conviction that, through the experience of power through faith in Christ, human beings were transformed in a way that was hitherto impossible. That fundamental conviction dominated Paul's reflections and exhortations about ethical issues.

Flowing from that conviction were several values which remained essential parts of his positions on various ethical questions presented to him during his missionary travels. Those two values were freedom and community. On the one hand, faith in Christ empowered Christians with a new freedom that allowed them to be and to act in a way that had previously been impossible. On the other hand, faith in Christ also made them members of a new community, and membership in that community involved the responsibility to seek the good of the other members and the good of the community as a whole. These two values, freedom and community, are the values that underlie the various ethical decisions that Paul made about his own life and the ethical decisions that he urged on the communities with which he comes in contact.

Yet these values can be in conflict with one another. This conflict is not between an irresponsible freedom to do what one knows to be wrong and an oppressive community that demands a mindless adhesion to even the smallest details of conduct. Paul knew that conflicts of that sort existed. Yet those kinds of conflicts were relatively easy to sort out.

For example, in 1 Corinthians 5:1-8 Paul was faced with a situation in which one of the members of the Christian community at Corinth had married his stepmother. To make matters worse, other Corinthian Christians boasted of this incestuous relationship, probably on the grounds that it was an example of the freedom that Christians had in Christ (see 1 Cor 5:6). Paul quite clearly condemned this irresponsible abuse of Christian freedom and demanded the excommunication of the offending party. Yet, at the same time, Paul was deeply committed to the value of true Christian freedom. At times he was loath to command even what he thought he had a right to command (see Phlm 8).

The real issues for Paul lay in balancing the conflicting values of legitimate Christian freedom and the equally legitimate needs of the Christian community. By looking at situations in which Paul dealt with those conflicts, one gains a much more specific sense of how Paul himself lived and how he thought Christians living in a Christian community ought to live. By looking at Paul's practice, one puts flesh and blood to the bare bones of "freedom" and "community" in the abstract.

Christian Responsibility in a Community

One of the most detailed and nuanced treatments of this problem by Paul is found in 1 Corinthians 8—10. These three chapters deal with the question of whether or not Christians should be able to eat meat that had previously been offered in sacrifice to some Greek or Roman deity. At first it may seem odd to us that Paul felt it necessary to spend three chapters on this particular problem, a problem that from our perspective is of little or no significance. Yet once one understands the situation in the Corinthian community to which Paul was writing and the social and religious background of that problem, it becomes clear why he spent so much effort in trying to offer a nuanced solution to the problem.

At first the issue seems simple enough. Should Christians be allowed to eat meat offered to idols? Some members of the Christian community at Corinth thought that the answer was obviously "yes." They argued that, as Christians, they had the knowledge to understand that "an idol has no real existence" (1 Cor 8:4), that is, there is no god behind that idol. If that is the case, sacrifices to idols mean nothing, and so meat offered in such sacrifices can be eaten without any qualms of conscience.

Their arguments certainly make a good deal of sense to us who are firmly convinced that there is only one God and that the eating of meat really offered to other "gods" is a meaningless question. Yet the situation of first-century Christians was much more complicated than that, especially when it is understood against its religious and social background.

Most of the Corinthian Christians were probably converts to Christianity from various Graeco-Roman cults. But they were still living in an environment in which the vast majority of their friends, neighbors, and even families were still active members of those cults. Sacrifice played an important role in those Graeco-Roman religious cults. The meat that was sacrificed in these cults was often then consumed by the worshippers who had made the sacrifice. In the Graeco-Roman world, these worshippers often formed associations organized as burial societies or along vocational lines. These societies or associations often held their sacrificial meals within the temple precincts of the appropriate god or goddess. The god or goddess to whom the sacrifice had been offered was thought to be present in a special way at these meals at which the sacrificial meat was eaten. The meat that was not eaten in this way was often sold in the markets of the city. This meant that much of the meat that was sold in the markets was meat that had previously been offered to some deity.

In this situation, the Corinthian Christians could confess, as Christians, that "there is no God but one" (1 Cor 8:4; see Deut 6:4); but their own religious pasts as well as the environment in which they lived made it very difficult to maintain that position in a thoroughgoing way. This meant that, when they saw other Christians eating meat offered to idols, they were strongly tempted to believe that these Christians were eating meat that had been really sacrificed to real gods. This act, which for some Christians was a matter of indifference, was for others an occasion for deep scandal.

The matter is further complicated when one also looks at the social rather than the religious background of the situation. In the ancient world, meat was not nearly as common a food as it is in the contemporary Western world. Meat was a very expensive commodity and, by and large, was reserved for the wealthy. The less well-off had very little meat in their diets. Most of the people who had access to meat or to meals at which meat was regularly served were members of the wealthier classes. This meant that those members of the Christian community at Corinth who had the opportunity to buy meat or who were invited to attend sacrificial meals where meat was served were among the wealthier minority of the Christian community there. Those members of the community, however, who were scandalized by the actions of those who had the means to obtain meat previously offered to a god or goddess were probably among the poorer majority. In other words, the problem that Paul was writing about was not simply a question of religious sensibilities; it also involved to some extent the social stratification of the Christian community at Corinth.

The problem that Paul was addressing, then, was more complex than it first appeared. In addition, it becomes clearer why the problem was of such significance to Paul. At stake were the religious convictions and sensibilities of many members of the Christian community about their fundamental belief in one God. With this background in mind one can now look at the rather complex way in which Paul deals with this problem.

Paul's argument about eating meat offered to idols can be divided up in the following manner:

8:1-13   Statement of problem and general principles: Knowledge versus adaptation to a weaker conscience.

9:1-27   The example of Paul's own missionary prac-

	tice: He does not exercise his right to be supported.
10:1-13	The warning example of the Israelites in the wilderness.
10:14-22	The Lord's Supper as a criterion: "You cannot drink the cup of the Lord and the cup of demons."
10:23-30	General stipulations about private conduct.
10:31—11:1	Conclusion: "Be imitators of me, as I am of Christ."

In the first section (8:1-13) Paul is concerned with describing the problem as he sees it and setting out the principles he wants to use in solving the dispute. He begins by quoting a slogan used by some of the Corinthian Christians: "all of us possess knowledge" (8:1). This was undoubtedly the slogan used by those who argued that, because they *knew* that there was only one God, sacrifices offered to idols were meaningless and so eating meat offered to idols was a matter of indifference. Paul concedes that they are right in the sense that "an idol has no real existence," and that "there is no God but one." But he then points out that knowledge puffs up, but love builds up (8:1). He suggests that there is a more fundamental value than knowledge, and that value is love. It is that value that will guide Paul's reflections on this conflict.

In 1 Corinthians 8:7-13 he describes more specifically how that value should supersede some of the Corinthian Christians' quite legitimate "knowledge" that there is but one God. He argues that not all Christians possess the knowledge that some of the Corinthian Christians claim to have. Some Christians, who were accustomed to the worship of a number of gods and goddesses prior to their conversions, are scandalized by some of their fellow Christians' eating meat offered to idols. Granted that their consciences are "weak," nevertheless this freedom that some Christians feel about eating meat offered to idols has become a stumbling block to their fellow Christians. Paul asks rhetorically: "For if any one sees you, a man of knowledge, at table in an idol's temple, might he not be encouraged, if his conscience is weak, to eat food offered to idols" (1 Cor 8:10)? The result is that by "knowledge" one could destroy a weak person, a brother or sister for whom Christ died. Paul's conclusion is that if food becomes the cause of another Christian's falling, then he will never eat meat (8:13). The good of a fellow Christian takes precedence over the otherwise legitimate claim to know that idols have no real existence.

The second section (9:1-27) is a discussion of Paul's missionary practice. He uses his own experience to illustrate how he worked out in his own missionary activity this principle of not standing on one's legitimate rights when the good of one's fellow Christians is involved. He begins by describing his own right as a missionary to support from Christian communities (9:1-12a). He claims that, as an apostle, he has the same rights as other apostles. Among those rights is the right to be supported in his missionary activities. He claims that this right is not of simply human authority. He quotes the Mosaic Law to substantiate his claim: "You shall not muzzle an ox when it is treading out the grain" (Deut 25:4). He argues that this passage was not meant to pertain only to oxen being allowed to eat while carrying out their work. Rather, it pertains primarily to those who are involved in a spiritual sowing and harvesting. Those sowing spiritual good have an even greater claim to receive material benefits in return.

But, Paul then goes on to emphasize that he has never made use of this right. In fact, he would rather die than make use of it. He boasts that he has made the gospel free of charge, that he has not made full use of his right in the gospel (9:12b-18). He then explains his motivation for not standing on his right to be supported in his missionary activities (9:19-23). He wants to be all things to all persons in order to save some of them. He has become a Jew to the Jews, that is, as one under the Law, even though he himself is not under the Law. To those outside of the Law, he has become as one outside the Law, even though he is under the "law" of Christ. Paul's point is not that he becomes a chameleon-like figure who changes his colors to suit the scenery. Rather, he is willing to adapt to different situations, if that adaptation is for the good of those for whom he is laboring. He then applies that principle to the situation at hand: "To the weak I became weak, that I might win the weak" (8:22). He uses the term "weak" at this point because that is the term that he used earlier (8:7, 9-11) to describe those who were scandalized at eating meat offered to idols.

Paul makes use of this example of his own missionary practice for several reasons. First, as we have seen before, Paul tries to root his arguments in experience, his own experience and the experience of those to whom he is writing. In this case, his own missionary activities in Corinth were not a burden to the Corinthians. Paul supported himself. He implies that their own positive experience of him was due in part to the fact that he supported himself and was not a burden to them, even though he had a right to their material support. They them-selves, then, have experienced the value of not insisting on the exercise of an otherwise legitimate right.

Second, Paul wants to use the force of his own conduct as an example of how the Corinthian Christians ought to act. At the end of his reflections on the question of eating meat offered to idols, he will exhort them to be imitators of him as he is of Christ (11:1). He feels that his own conduct should be an example to them, just as Christ's conduct was an example for him.

This section of 1 Corinthians certainly contributes to Paul's argument about concern for the consciences of one's fellow Christians. But it also gives us a glimpse into how Paul understood who he was and how he was to act. His own deep commitment to Christ relativized other legitimate values. He had a sense of what was, and in this case what was not, central to that commitment. Not everything was of equal importance. As a matter of fact, everything was to be seen in the light of Christ's concern for even the weak Christian. Just as Paul relativized the value of the Mosaic Law in the light of his belief in the universal significance of Christ's death and resurrection, so too he now relativized the importance of knowledge when acting on that knowledge would be harmful to his fellow Christians.

Paul turns in the next section (10:1-13) from the example of his own conduct among the Corinthian Christians to interpretations of passages from the Pentateuch. As he often does, after recalling their own experience, Paul then turns to interpretations of scripture to deepen his arguments. Once again, he appeals first to experience and then to tradition.

He begins by recalling to their minds passages from the Pentateuch about Israel's Exodus from Egypt and its wandering for forty years in the desert.

> [1]I want you to know, brethren, that our fathers were all under the cloud, and all passed through the sea, [2]and all were baptized into Moses in the cloud and in the sea, [3]and all ate the same spiritual food [4]and all drank the same spiritual drink. For they drank from the spiritual Rock which followed them, and the Rock was Christ. [5]Nevertheless with most of them God was not pleased; for they were overthrown in the wilderness. [6]Now these things are types for us, so that we do not desire evil as they did. (1 Cor 10:1-6)

Paul is engaging here in a type of interpretation that seems very odd to us. He appears to be reading Christian symbols into these passages from the Old Testament, and he appears to be doing it in a very arbitrary manner. Yet he is using a kind of interpretation very popular among Jews of his own day, a kind of interpretation that will be equally popular among early Christians. This is a figurative or allegorical interpretation of the Bible. The assumption behind it is that the biblical text has multiple levels of meaning. Beyond the straightforward, literal meaning of the text exists a deeper, more universal meaning. This deeper, more universal meaning, while it does not cancel out the literal meaning, does go well beyond it. In this way, Paul and many of his contemporaries thought that the biblical text, in a veiled or figurative way, pointed to realities which were deeper and more universal than the realities described at the surface of the text.

In Paul's case, these figurative meanings hidden in the biblical text point to the specifically Christian realities of baptism and the eucharist. In a figurative way, Israel's being guided by the pillar of cloud (Exod 13:21) and passing through the sea (Exod 14:22) point to Christian baptism. In a similar way, Israel's eating of the manna (Exod 16:4-35) and drinking from the rock (Exod 17:65; Num 20:7-11) point to the Christian eucharist. In fact, Paul seems to identify the rock from which the Israelites drank with Christ (1 Cor 10:4). The point Paul is making here is not that the pre-existent Christ was the rock which provided the Israelites with water. Rather, the context of this passage is figurative, that is, the rock which provided water for the Israelites figuratively, in a veiled way, corresponds to the nourishment provided by Christ in the eucharist.

Paul then goes on to interpret the experience of Israel in the wilderness in a similarly figurative way as an example of how Christians ought not to act. In this way, the figurative example becomes a veiled warning for Christians (1 Cor 8: 5-13). In the wilderness, the Israelites practiced idolatry by worshipping the golden calf (Exod 32:4, 6); they indulged in immorality of various sorts and were killed for it (Num 25: 1-18); they put the Lord to the test by challenging Moses' motivation for bringing them out of Egypt and were slain by serpents (Num 21:5-6); others grumbled against Moses and died in a plague (Num 16:14, 49).

The point that is implied in Paul's description of all of these events is that, even though the Israelites had passed through the sea and eaten the spiritual food (prefigurements of Christian baptism and the eucharist), they had still incurred God's wrath by their immoral and irresponsible bahavior. The Corinthian Christians, then, must beware lest their own conduct lead to their downfall. It was no accident that the first crime of the Israelites in the wilderness that Paul lists is that of idolatry, the worship of the golden calf. He seems to imply that with questions of idolatry, one must be very careful, and that what happened to the Israelites in the desert should put the

Corinthian Christians on their guard.

In the next section (10:14-22) Paul turns from the interpretation of the Old Testament to a consideration of the symbolism of the Christian eucharist. Paul begins by reminding the Corinthian Christians that the cup of blessing that they bless is a participation in the blood of Christ and that the bread that they break is a participation in the body of Christ (10:16). For Christians, participation in the eucharistic meal is a participation in Christ.

He then compares participation in that meal with participation in sacrificial meals eaten in honor of other gods. He does not want the Corinthian Christians to misunderstand him. He is not claiming that food offered to idols is anything or that the idols themselves are anything. Nevertheless, participation in such meals does involve the Christian in a rite that Paul thinks of as offering sacrifices to demons.

In making this claim, Paul once again appeals to the witness of scripture. He appeals especially to sections of the Song of Moses in Deuteronomy 32. In these passages Moses castigates the Israelites for their conduct in the wilderness. In the wilderness, they sacrificed to demons which were no gods (Deut 32:17), and for this reason they stirred the Lord to jealousy with what was no god (Deut 32:21). Paul warns the Corinthian Christians not to risk the same fate. He rhetorically warns them: You cannot drink the cup of the Lord and the cup of demons; You cannot partake of the table of the Lord and the table of demons (10:21).

In this section Paul is warning some of the Corinthian Christians against a specific practice that some of them seem to have been involved in. Some of them seem to have accepted invitations from non-Christian friends and neighbors to participate in meals in temple precincts, meals where meat was eaten which had been offered to a god or goddess. There is no indication that they participated in the sacrifices themselves; but they did participate in the meals eaten afterwards. Paul was opposed, however, to such a practice because, in his mind, it amounted to participation in the sacrifice offered to the god or goddess.

Paul is careful to emphasize that this god or goddess is no real god; there is but one God. But, as we saw earlier, Paul believed that these "gods" and "goddesses" did exist. They were not God; they were demons. They were the "rulers of this age" and were involved in the crucifixion of Jesus (1 Cor 2:8). Once a person had become a Christian, these demons no longer had any power over the person. Nevertheless they still existed, and by participating in meals in honor of these demons, Christians were in effect placing themselves once again under their power (cf. Gal 4:8-10). For this reason, Paul was completely opposed to such a practice.

In the final section (10:23-30), Paul deals with two other situations which involve eating meat that had previously been offered to idols. The general principle that Paul makes use of here is the one that he used at the beginning of his reflections on this issue: "Let no one seek his own good, but the good of his neighbor" (10:23). The first of these situations is that of buying meat at the meat market and eating it in the privacy of one's own home. In Paul's mind this situation should cause no problem. Such meat can be eaten with a clear conscience. No question need be raised because the situation does not involve harming the conscience of one's fellow Christian. He quotes Psalm 24:1: "the earth is the Lord's and everything in it."

The second situation is more complex. If unbelievers invite

Christians to a meal in their home, they are free to go. They are also free to eat whatever is served at the meal. They are free to do so, Paul implies, because the meal is not at a temple precinct and so is not understood by the Christians' hosts as participation in a sacrifice offered to some god or goddess.

If someone at the meal, however, makes a point of remarking to a Christian that the meat at the meal had been previously offered in sacrifice, then the Christian should refrain from eating it. It is not clear from the context of this section whether the person who had raised the issue is a Christian or not. One suspects, however, that Paul assumes that the person asking the question is a Christian, since the whole context of the discussion of 1 Corinthians 8—10 is the problem of scandal given to other Christians. In any case, Paul warns against eating meat in such circumstances.

He makes it very clear though that the reason for not eating the meat is not because eating such meat is inherently wrong. Rather, it is because one should not harm the other person's conscience (10:28-29). Paul, then, returns to the place where he began, the importance of not exercising a legitimate right, when such an exercise would harm a fellow Christian. At the same time, however, Paul emphasizes the fact that, if fellow Christians' consciences are not involved, then one has a perfect right to make use of the freedom one has as a Christian.

Paul concludes this section (10:31—11:1) with an exhortation to the Corinthian Christians to be imitators of him as he is of Christ in seeking not his own advantage but that of the many so that many may be saved (10:33).

In his advice and warnings to the Corinthian Christians about the problem of eating meat offered to idols, Paul's paramount concern was for the consciences of the "weaker brethren," a concern lest they be harmed by other Christians exercising an otherwise legitimate right that they had as Christians. He was, however, writing to those Christians who thought of themselves as "strong," Christians who claimed to be in the know. He was warning them against arrogantly imposing their "knowledge" on other Christians.

Christian Freedom

While Paul seems to have limited the exercise of Christian freedom in his treatment of the question of meat offered to idols, he seems to have taken the opposite tack when dealing with questions of marriage and celibacy in 1 Corinthians 7. If he emphasizes Christian responsibility in 1 Corinthians 8-10, in 1 Corinthians 7 he emphasized Christian freedom.

While Paul's emphasis on Christian freedom in 1 Corinthians 7 has a great deal of appeal to us, certain sections in this chapter strike us as rather odd. This is especially the case when Paul advises the Corinthian Christians against marriage (1 Cor 7:25-40). Yet one has to be aware of the reasons that Paul has for giving such advice. As we shall see, those reasons have to do with Paul's expectations about the return of Christ in power in the near future, an expectation that Paul shared with many other early Christians.

1 Corinthians 7 is divided into several sections, and these different sections deal with different aspects of marriage and celibacy.

7:1-7   General observations about the married state and its obligations.

7:8-16	Specific advice to widowers and widows (8-9), to the married (10-11), to those married to non-believers (12-16).
7:17-24	Eschatological freedom: "Let everyone lead the life which the Lord has assigned to him."
7:25-40	Advice given not to marry in view of the present or impending distress.

Paul begins his reflections and advice about marriage and celibacy with some general observations (1 Cor 7:1-7). These observations take issue with a viewpoint evidently espoused by some of the Corinthian Christians (1 Cor 7:1-2).

> ¹Now concerning the matters about which you wrote. "It is well for a man not to touch a woman." ²But because of the temptation to immorality, each man should have his own wife and each woman her own husband.

The Corinthian Christians wrote to Paul asking him questions about a number of issues. The issue of marriage and celibacy was the first of these issues. As he will do in 1 Cor 8—10, Paul begins by stating the position that some of the Corinthian Christians seem to have adopted. Their position is that "it is well for a man not to touch a woman." Some of the Corinthian Christians came to the conclusion that Christians should not marry and that even those who are married should refrain from sexual intercourse.

It is not clear how these Corinthian Christians came to such a conclusion. One explanation is that they, like Paul, expected the second coming of Christ to be soon. Since that second coming was going to be preceded by tribulation, Christians should not be entangled in anything that was of this world. In this they may have claimed that Paul was on their side.

There is, however, a more likely explanation. At least some of the Corinthian Christians do not seem to have had such an expectation. From 1 Corinthians 15 it appears that some of the Corinthian Christians did not believe in the resurrection of the dead. Rather, Christians, by the very fact that they were Christians, were already "resurrected." All they had to do was to await death, which was nothing more than the sloughing off of the body. They were already living a resurrected life. If that was the case, then one should have as little to do with the body and its pleasures as possible. Specifically, one should not marry and, even if already married, one should not engage in sexual intercourse.

Paul, however, takes a quite different position. Because of the "temptation to immorality," Christian men and women should be married. Each man should have his own wife, and each woman her own husband. In addition, both the man and the woman should give to the other his or her conjugal rights. As a rule, they should not refrain from having sexual intercourse with each other. They may agree to do so for a short period of time in order to devote themselves to prayer. But that situation should only be temporary. Even refraining from sexual intercourse for that short period of time is understood by Paul as a concession and not as a command.

Paul's characterization of the motivation for Christians' marrying, the "temptation to immorality," may strike us as a rather poor reason for marriage. Marriage, after all, should be rooted primarily in the love between a man and a woman rather than in sexual desire. One explanation for Paul's attitude may have been his belief that Christ's second coming was imminent and that it would be preceded by tribulation. In view of that tribulation, Christians would be better off not becoming involved in marriage (7:25-35).

As we shall see, this may explain Paul's advice to unmarried Christians not to get married, but it does not explain his description of the motivation for marriage as avoiding "temptation to immorality." Even in this chapter Paul describes marriage in terms of husband and wife trying to please one another, and it is clear that he is not primarily thinking of "pleasing" in a sexual sense (7:32-35). He is thinking of the mutual concern that husband and wife have for one another. Paul himself, then, does not otherwise think of marriage as primarily a way of avoiding temptations to immorality.

A more likely reason for Paul's use of the phrase "temptation to immorality" is that it too was a term used by the Corinthian Christians who thought that Christians should refrain from marrying and, if married, should refrain from having sexual intercourse with each other. Paul counters the Corinthians' argument by claiming that even the "temptation to immorality," rather than being a reason not to marry, is a reason for Christians to be married. This explanation fits better both with Paul's own description of marriage later in this chapter and with the attitudes of the Corinthian Christians against which Paul is writing.

What is more important, however, is the way in which Paul makes his arguments. It brings out a crucial aspect of Paul's ethical practice. Some of the Corinthian Christians were in essence trying to forbid Christians to marry. Their position was a kind of perfectionism. Paul, however, takes the opposite position. Christians are free to marry; and, in fact, most should marry. Couples could refrain from sexual intercourse for a time in order to be devoted to prayer, but then they should resume their normal sexual activities. In essence, Paul is opting for Christian freedom.

The extent to which Paul is committed to this freedom becomes clearer when one realizes that Paul himself wished that all of the Corinthian Christians would be as he was, that is, unmarried (7:7). Yet, he adds, "but each has his own special gift from God, one of one kind and one of another" (7:7). This means that for him to be unmarried is a gift of God; yet it is also a gift of God for other Christians to be married. Paul will make use of this principle throughout the rest of this chapter. When it comes to God's gifts to different individuals, Paul feels free to offer advice, but he does not feel that he has any right to give commands.

In the next section (7:8-16) Paul puts this principle into practice in three different cases: widowers and widows, the married, and those involved in marriages to non-Christians.

In the case of widowers and widows (7:8-9), Paul advises them to remain as he is, that is, unmarried. The Revised Standard Version translates this section as advice "to the *unmarried (agamois)* and the widows." Since, however, Paul will deal with the question of those who have never been married (*parthenon*) in 7:25-28, it makes more sense to take the word *agamois* in 7:8 to mean "*presently* unmarried" rather than to mean "*never* married." The word is then parallel with the word for widows (*cherais*) and so probably means "widowers." But if they cannot exercise self-control, then they should re-marry. Paul offers advice but he carefully refrains from issuing any commands.

Paul's words to those who are already married (7:10-11) are of a different sort. It is not he but the Lord who charges

Christian husbands and wives not to separate from one another. But if they do separate from one another, they are to remain single or be reconciled to one another. In this section Paul is referring to a saying of Jesus found in Mark 10:11-12 and Luke 16:18. Because it is a saying of the Lord, Paul does not feel free simply to offer advice; he gives them a command.

Yet that command is not one that is without exceptions, and those exceptions are made by Paul. This becomes clear when one looks at the advice given by Paul to those Christians who are married to non-Christians (7:12-16). Paul's advice is that if a Christian marries a non-Christian and that non-Christian consents to remain with the Christian spouse, then the Christian partner should not divorce the non-Christian. If, however, the non-Christian partner wants to separate, then Paul allows the separation to take place. Paul gives as justification for this practice the belief that "God has called us to peace" (7:15). What is interesting in this passage is that Paul, in the name of peace, thinks that he can limit the scope of a saying of the Lord. He himself admits that this advice comes from him and not from the Lord (7:12). Even a saying of the Lord cannot be applied unconditionally; it too allows for exceptions when the peace to which God has called Christians is endangered by applying the saying.

In the next section (7:17-24), Paul steps back for a moment from the particular questions that he has been dealing with and offers more general reflections in order to put his advice in a larger context. At the beginning and at the end of this section he offers a general principle:

> [17]Only, let every one lead the life which the Lord has assigned to him, and in which God has called him. This is my rule in all the

churches. . . ²⁴So, brethren, in whatever state each was called, there let him remain with God. (1 Cor 7:17, 24)

He then offers two examples. If at the time of one's call, that is, at the time one became a Christian, one was circumcised, let him not remove the marks of circumcision. If, on the other hand, one was not circumcised, let him not become circumcised. If one was a slave at the time of one's call, let him remain in that state, unless one is given the opportunity to become a freedman.

In each case, the justification is basically the same. Neither circumcision nor uncircumcision counts for anything, but keeping the commandments of God does. If a Christian is a slave, he is a freedman in Christ; if he is free, he is still a "slave" of Christ. Paul's point is that what is crucial is one's faith in Christ and the experience that comes with that faith. Everything else is secondary, and so one should not be obsessed with these secondary matters.

In the context of this chapter of 1 Corinthians, Paul seems to be trying to make the Corinthian Christians understand that their perfectionist tendencies about not marrying are leading them to absolutize what is of secondary importance. God has called people in various states of life, circumcised and uncircumcised, slave and free, married and unmarried. Concern about altering those states should not become an excuse for creating social havoc within the Christian community.

Once he has made this general point, Paul then returns in the final section of this chapter (7:25-40) to the question of those who have never been married. He begins by reiterating the principle that he developed in 7:17-24 that "it is well for a person to remain as he is" (7:26). The reason for this is the impending distress. Paul believes that the appointed time before the return of the Lord is short (7:29). Because of that, Christians should not seek to change their social situation or become too attached to it.

Within this context Paul offers his advice to those who have never been married. He advises them not to marry. He makes it perfectly clear to them that he is not giving them a command of the Lord; it is only advice, advice which he thinks is trustworthy, but which is still only advice. The reason for offering this particular advice is that the married man and the married woman are inevitably concerned with pleasing each other. That very legitimate concern for each other can become, especially in the troubles and tribulations that will precede the coming of Christ in power, a cause of anxiety that distracts both of them from concern for the coming of the Lord.

Paul is very careful about the way in which he gives this advice: "I say this for your own benefit, not to lay any restraint upon you, but to promote good order and to secure your undivided attention to the Lord" (7:35). If Christians, however, decide to marry, there is nothing wrong with that (7:28). In fact they do well; but those who refrain from marriage do better (7:38).

The portrait of Paul that emerges from a careful reading of the often tortuous arguments of this chapter is of someone who is firmly convinced that he knows what is best, who has, as he says, the Spirit of God (7:40). But the portrait is equally of one who is unwilling to impose that conviction on other Christians, who is unwilling to inhibit the freedom to which God has called other Christians. In this chapter he is defending the legitimate exercise of Christian freedom.

Conclusion

At the surface level, Paul's handling of the situations in 1 Corinthians 7 stands in contrast to his handling of the situations in 1 Corinthians 8-10. In 1 Corinthians 8-10 he strongly counseled some of the Corinthian Christians against exercising their legitimate freedom to eat meat that had been offered to idols. In 1 Corinthians 7 he encourages just such an exercise of legitimate Christian freedom. There is a certain tension between Christian freedom and the needs of the Christian community. The tension, however, is more apparent than real. What underlies Paul's treatment of both sets of situations is a conviction rooted once again in the contrast of strength and weakness. Christians who claim to be "strong" (either by exercising the freedom to eat meat offered to idols or the freedom not to marry) must be very careful not to impose their will on other, perhaps "weaker," Christians or to act in a way that would bring ruin on those Christians. Paul's ethical practice is dominated by the belief that in Christ one can be strong, and that that strength allows one to refrain from imposing one's own convictions on the practice of other Christians. Deeply imbedded in one's Christian freedom is that most difficult of freedoms, the freedom from feeling compelled to make others always act in the way that one thinks that they should act. It is the freedom that allows one to recognize that God has called different Christians in different ways.

7

SUFFERING AND HOPE
FOR THE FUTURE

"That, to the height of this great argument, I may assert Eternal Providence, and justify the ways of God to men" was the way that John Milton (1608-1674) described his purpose at the beginning of *Paradise Lost*. He tried to show how belief in an all-good God could be reconciled with the obvious and terrifying fact of human suffering and death. Milton has given us the classic definition of theodicy, the vindication of the justice of God in permitting evil to exist.

While Milton may have given to English literature its classic formulation, the problem of reconciling the existence of evil, of human suffering and death, with the belief in an omnipotent and loving God is much older than Milton. In one form or another, the problem is as old as humankind itself. Attempted solutions to the problem of evil, or perhaps more accurately the mystery of evil, are almost as old.

The Background of the Old Testament

We find such a solution attempted at the very beginning of the Bible. In Genesis 3 we read of the story of the sin of the first human beings, Adam and Eve. The story is not about an "original sin" whose consequences were then passed on physically to all future generations. Rather, the story was meant to show that the existence of evil and death was not the result of God's original plan but of disobedience on the part of human beings. The cause of evil in the world was to be laid at our doorstep. Human choice and not divine providence is the cause of evil. This same basic conviction is developed in the rest of the stories of Genesis 4—11 (e.g., the murder of Abel, Noah and the Ark, and the Tower of Babel). Wrong human choices have led to evil consequences for all of humanity.

That same conviction about the evil consequences of wrong human decisions is also found in the wisdom literature of the Old Testament. But this conviction is balanced by a second conviction, that wise human choices lead to good consequences. For the book of Proverbs, there is a kind of balance in the world. If one acts wisely, one will prosper; if one acts foolishly, one will suffer because of one's foolishness. There is an order to the world, and, if one violates that order, one will suffer because of that violation.

In addition, the prosperity that one experiences is commensurate with one's wise choices, and one's suffering is commensurate with one's foolish choices. The world is an ordered place and there is a balance between one's actions and the consequences of those actions. This balance is achieved within this present world. The viewpoint of most of wisdom literature is a thoroughly this-worldly vision. While challenged especially by the poetic section of the book of Job (Job 3:1—42:6), this view probably represented the common conviction of much of the literature of the Old Testament.

Apocalypticism in Judaism, Early Christianity, and Paul

The real challenge to this viewpoint, however, came not from the author of the poetic section of Job but from events in the history of Israel and their interpretation. While it is difficult, if not impossible, to pinpoint its origins, several groups within Israel, by the end of the third century B.C., came to believe that the world was fundamentally not an orderly place but was filled with disorder. That disorder was so deep-seated that the world could not be righted by the usual interaction of innerworldly forces. The balance could not be restored in the usual way. It required an intervention by God.

While not the earliest expression of this belief, the most well known is found in the book of Daniel, which was written during the Maccabean revolt (167-64 B.C.). In a revelatory vision (an apocalypse), Daniel saw a series of successive world empires, the last of which (the Seleucid Empire of Antiochus IV) has gone completely out of control and has even desecrated the Temple in Jerusalem (Dan 11:2-45). Order can no longer be restored by the interaction of innerworldly forces; a divine intervention by God on behalf of the just is required. This intervention is described in Dan 12:1-3:

> [1]At that time shall arise Michael the great prince who has charge of your people (i.e., Israel). And there shall be a great time of

trouble, such as never has been since there was a nation till that time; but at that time your people shall be delivered, every one whose name shall be found written in the book. [2]And many of those who sleep in the dust of the earth shall awake, some to everlasting life, and some to shame and everlasting contempt. [3]And those who are wise shall shine like the brightness of the firmament; and those who turn many to righteousness, like the stars for ever and ever.

Four elements in this revelatory or apocalyptic vision are important for understanding the viewpoint of early Christianity and of Paul about human suffering and the vindication of the just. First, God's vindication of the just will take place only after a period of great suffering. Second, that vindication will involve an intervention by God. Third, since such a vindication has become impossible within this life, it will take place through a resurrection of the dead, a resurrection in which the just will be eternally rewarded and the wicked eternally punished. Finally, all of this process, both the suffering and the vindication, were expected to take place in the near future.

This apocalyptic viewpoint found in some groups within early Judaism was taken over by early Christians. The most significant alteration made by early Christians was their belief that Jesus would be the one who would be God's agent in this vindication of the just, in this case the Christians. The role played by the angel Michael in Daniel was played by Jesus' coming in power for the early Christians. This conviction gave them hope in the face of the sufferings that they were experiencing.

Paul too shared this conviction about the imminent coming of Christ in power. In 1 Thessalonians, the earliest of Paul's letters, Paul describes his preaching to the Thessalonians and how they turned to God from idols, to serve a living and true God, and to wait for his Son from heaven, whom God raised from the dead, Jesus, who delivers them from the wrath to come (1 Thess 1:9-10). Behind this preaching lies an outlook deeply affected by an apocalyptic vision of Jesus returning in power to deliver Christians from their sufferings and to punish the wicked.

This outlook becomes even clearer later in the letter when Paul faces the problem of what will become of those Christians who have died before Jesus' return in power. Will they be at a disadvantage? Paul consoles the Thessalonian Christians with the following words:

> [13]But we would not have you ignorant, brethren, concerning those who are asleep, that you may not grieve as others do who have no hope. [14]For since we believe that Jesus died and rose again, even so, through Jesus, God will bring with him those who have fallen asleep. [15]For this we declare to you by the word of the Lord, that we who are alive, who are left until the coming of the Lord, shall not precede those who have fallen asleep. [16]For the Lord himself will descend from heaven with a cry of command, with the archangel's call, and with the sound of the trumpet of God. And the dead in Christ will rise first; [17]then we who are alive, who are left, shall be caught up together with them in the clouds to meet the Lord in the air; and so we shall always be with the Lord. [18]Therefore comfort one another with these words. (1 Thess 4:13-18)

Like the apocalyptic vision of Daniel, Paul's words were meant to offer consolation to those Christians whose family and friends had already died. This consolation in the face of suffering and death evoked a vision of Jesus' returning in power and raising the dead to new life and joining them to those who were still alive. From 1 Thessalonians 4:15 ("we who are alive, who are left until the coming of the Lord"), it is clear that Paul expected that Jesus' coming in power would happen in the near future.

Paul's expectation of Jesus' returning soon in power is also reflected in his advice in 1 Corinthians 7 to the unmarried not to marry, a passage that we looked at when we considered Paul's ethical practice. In that passage Paul advised unmarried Christians not to marry because of the suffering that they were experiencing or about to experience (1 Cor 7:26). For Paul, the "form of this world is passing away" (1 Cor 7:31).

Universal Hope for the Future

The framework, then, of Paul's convictions about the relationship of suffering to future consolation or vindication is very much in continuity with that of other early Christians. At the same time, his own thoughts on human suffering and Christian hope develop in directions that go beyond the traditional views that he received and passed on. From the point of view of a spirituality, two of those directions are most important. The first concerns the inclusiveness and universality of his hopes for the future. The second concerns the ways in which he came to understand the role played by present suffering in his Christian vision.

As one reads the apocalyptic vision in Daniel and Paul's own description of Jesus' return in power in 1 Thessalonians 1:9-10; 4:13-18, one is struck by the divisive character of the apocalyptic vision. The just will be vindicated, but all others will be condemned. One also has the sense that the number of those who are to be saved will be quite small, and the number of those condemned will be much larger. Those who will be saved are the true believers, the "wise" and "those who turn many to righteousness" in the case of Daniel, and Christians in the case of Paul. The "many" who are turned to righteousness in Daniel are still only a part of Israel and include no Gentiles; and the Christians of Paul's time made up only a small portion of humankind. In its traditional form the apocalyptic vision of the vindication of the just tends to be exclusive and not at all universal.

Although still sharing much of the imagery of early Jewish and Christian apocalyptic, Paul's hopes for the future take on a much more inclusive and universalistic coloration. Because many of Paul's images remain within the structure of this traditional apocalyptic vision, there is a tension in Paul's vision of the future between the narrower, traditional apocalyptic outlook and his own more universalistic and inclusive viewpoint. This more universal and inclusive vision of the future is found especially in two passages in Paul's letters, one in 1 Corinthians 15 and the other in Romans 8.

In 1 Corinthians 15 Paul tries to answer two questions raised by some of the Corinthian Christians: Is there a resurrection of the dead (1 Cor 15:12-34) and what will the resurrected body be like (1 Cor 15:35-49)? While the position taken by some of the Corinthian Christians is not completely clear, they seem to have claimed that they were already leading a resurrected life in virtue of their baptism. At death they would slough off their mortal bodies, but they looked forward to no further resurrection of the body. Paul's basic argument against them was to link the resurrection of the body to Christ's resurrection. If there was no resurrection of the body, then Christ could not have been raised; and if Christ had not been raised, then their faith was in vain (1 Cor 15:12-19). But Christ has been raised from the dead and so there must be a resurrection of the body (1 Cor 15:20).

In this context Paul talks about the consummation of the world, once from the viewpoint of Christ (1 Cor 15:20-28), and again a second time from the viewpoint of Christians (1 Cor 15:42-57). In 1 Corinthians 15:20-28 he begins with a reaffirmation of the resurrection of Christ and the relationship of that resurrection to the resurrection of the dead.

> [20]But in fact Christ has been raised from the dead, the first fruits of those who have fallen asleep. [21]For as by a man came death, by a man has come also the resurrection of the dead. [22]For as in Adam all die, so also in Christ shall all be made alive. [23]But each in his own order: Christ the first fruits, then at his coming those who believe in Christ. [24]Then comes the end, when he delivers the kingdom to God the Father after destroying every rule and every authority and power. [25]For he must reign until he has put all his enemies under his feet. [26]The last enemy to be destroyed is death.

In this passage the structure of traditional apocalyptic is maintained, especially in verse 23. Christ was the first to be raised; and, at his coming in power, all those who believe in Christ will be raised. The resurrection is limited to those who believe in Christ, a comparatively small group. Yet the language that surrounds this verse moves in a somewhat different direction. In 1 Corinthians 15:21-22 Paul sets Christ over against Adam. Through Adam death entered the world and death became universal (cf. Rom 5:1-20), but in Christ the dead are raised. The logic of the language moves in the direction of claiming that in Christ the resurrection of the dead is at least a universal possibility for all human beings. Just as in Adam death became a universal fact of human life, so in Christ the overcoming of death has now become a possibility for all.

The same emphasis on universality is found in 1 Corinthians 15:24-26. Christ will deliver the kingdom to God the Father after destroying every rule and authority and power, and the last of those is death. In this context, the rule, authority, and power are not human rulers or authorities but heavenly rulers and authorities, symbolized most clearly in death, all of which oppress human beings (cf. Gal 4:8-11; 1 Cor 2:6-9). It is noteworthy that nowhere in this list of enemies does Paul mention other human beings. In other words, Paul does not see those who do not believe in Christ as among those enemies who are to be destroyed. The enemies of Christ are not human enemies. This is rather different from the viewpoint of Daniel 12:1-3, where those who were not part of the group of the "wise" were to rise to everlasting contempt (Dan 12:2).

The same tension is also found in 1 Corinthians 15:42-56 when Paul talks more directly about the resurrection of the dead. Here he describes the contrast between the earthly body and the resurrected body.

> [42]So it is with the resurrection of the dead. What is sown is perishable, what is raised is imperishable. [43]It is sown in dishonor, it is raised in glory. It is sown in weakness, it is raised in power. [44]It is sown a physical body, it is raised a spiritual body. If there is a physical body, there is also a spiritual body. [45]Thus it is written, "The first man Adam became a living being" (Gen 2:7); the last Adam became a life-giving spirit. [46]But it is not the spiritual which is first but the physical, and then the spiritual.

> ⁴⁷The first man was from the earth, a man of dust; the second man is from heaven. ⁴⁸As was the man of dust, so are those who are of the dust; and as is the man of heaven, so are those who are of heaven. ⁴⁹Just as we have borne the image of the man of dust, we shall also bear the image of the man of heaven.
>
> (1 Cor 15:42-49)

Once again Paul introduces a comparison between Christ and Adam, and between those who are of Christ and those who are of Adam. On the one hand, this comparison introduces a division within humanity, between those who are of Christ and therefore of heaven, and those who are of Adam and therefore of dust (1 Cor 15:47-49). Yet within that same comparison, there is a more universal notion. If all of humanity is of Adam, that is, of dust, then all of humanity stands in need of redemption in Christ. Paul makes such an argument in Romans 1—3 and 5, and his conclusion is that in Christ such a redemption is possible for all human beings, whether Jew or Gentile. The comparison of Christ with Adam almost inevitably leads to a more universalistic and inclusive eschatology than is found in traditional Jewish or Christian apocalyptic.

This universalist element surfaces again in the highly rhetorical conclusion of 1 Corinthians 15. In 1 Corinthians 15:51-57, Paul once again talks about death as the final enemy to be overcome.

> ⁵¹Lo! I tell you a mystery. We shall not all sleep, but we shall all be changed, ⁵²in a moment, in the twinkling of an eye, at the last trumpet. For the trumpet will sound, and the dead will be raised imperishable, and we shall be changed. ⁵³For this perishable nature must put on the imperishable, and this mortal nature must put on immortality. ⁵⁴When the perishable puts on the imperishable, and the mortal puts on immortality, then shall

come to pass the saying that is written: "Death is swallowed up in victory." [55]"O death, where is thy victory? O death, where is thy sting?" [56]The sting of death is sin, and the power of sin is the law. [57]But thanks be to God, who gives us the victory through our Lord Jesus Christ.

While the imagery is very apocalyptic, the real enemy is not groups of human beings but death, the power that, along with sin, oppresses all of humanity. Paul's firm hope is that all of humanity will be delivered from that power. His thrust in the direction of the universality of salvation, while rooted in an apocalyptic outlook, moves well beyond it.

There is a tension, then, in Paul's thought between a vision of the consummation of the world which is limited to a relatively small group of believers and one which is much more universal and inclusive in outlook. This same tension is found in Romans 8, the other place in Paul's letters where he describes the consummation of the world.

Romans 8 contains Paul's description of the role of the Spirit in the lives of Christians. For Paul the Spirit empowers the Christian to overcome the powers of sin and death (Rom 8:1-17). The possession of the Spirit is also the Christian's hope of future glory. In this context, Paul offers another description of the consummation of the world.

[18]I consider that the sufferings of this present time are not worth comparing with the glory that is to be revealed to us. [19]For the creation waits with eager longing for the revealing of the sons of God; [20]for the creation was subjected to futility, not of its own will but by the will of him who subjected it in hope; [21]because the creation itself will be set free from its bondage to decay and obtain the glorious liberty of the children of God. [22]We know that the whole creation has been groaning in travail together

> until now; [23]and not only the creation, but we ourselves, who
> have the first fruits of the Spirit, groan inwardly as we wait for
> adoption as sons, the redemption of our bodies. (Rom 8:18-23)

He is obviously writing about the hopes that Christians have
about the future resurrection of the dead in glory. But he is
writing not simply about Christians but also about the consummation of the whole of creation. In describing the futility
to which all of creation has been subjected, Paul is drawing on
images also found in apocalyptic literature (2 *Apoc. Bar.* 15:8;
32:6; 4 *Ezra* 7:11, 75). But what he is emphasizing is the
universal and inclusive character of the consummation of the
world. In addition, in this passage from Romans Paul again
omits the mention of the punishment or destruction of any
group of human enemies. Paul's vision of the future does not
look to the final division of humanity into two groups, the
good and the evil. Rather it looks to a final consummation in
which all of those elements which are hostile to humanity are
finally overcome by the power of God in Christ. This viewpoint is expressed most eloquently at the very end of this
chapter:

> [38]For I am sure that neither death, nor life, nor angels, nor
> principalities, nor things present, nor things to come, nor
> powers, [39]nor height, nor depth, nor anything else in all creation,
> will be able to separate us from the love of God in Christ Jesus
> our Lord. (Rom 8:38-39)

The placing of this passage in Romans also gives us a clue
about why Paul turned traditional Christian apocalyptic
imagery in a more universal and inclusive direction. The
thrust of Paul's letter to the Romans was to defend his
preaching of the gospel to the Gentiles without the Law and to

clarify the problems that such preaching raised for certain Christians. In other words, Romans is an attempt to defend Paul's central conviction that in Christ both Jews and Gentiles were equally called to redemption. If the call was thus universalized, if the distinction between Jew and Gentile was abolished in Christ, then one's hope for the future likewise had to be universalized so as to include the Gentiles. Paul's own basic convictions led him to move beyond the division of humanity into two hostile groups to a more unified image of the consummation of the world.

The Meaning and Value of Present Suffering

Paul's own understanding of the role of suffering in the lives of Christians underwent a similar development. Just as the development of his thought about the hopes that Christians have for the future moved beyond the traditional Jewish and early Christian apocalyptic viewpoint, so too his understanding of the place of suffering in Christian life moved beyond the way in which suffering was understood in those circles.

In this traditional apocalyptic viewpoint, suffering was rewarded when the end of the age came. It is best illustrated again by Daniel 12:1-3. At the end of the age, there will be a time of great trouble and suffering. Then there will be a resurrection of the dead. The just will rise to everlasting life and will shine like the brightness of the firmament. But the unjust will rise to shame and everlasting contempt. Suffering, then, is something experienced by the just which will be vindicated and rewarded. In this apocalyptic viewpoint, suffering takes on its meaning because those who suffer will be vindicated in the future, at the end of the age.

We also find this viewpoint in Paul. In 1 Thessalonians 1:2-10 Paul describes the way in which the Thessalonian Christians have received and practiced what Paul had preached to them. He points out that they received the word in much affliction (1 Thess 1:6). He then goes on to assure them that their awaiting of Jesus' coming in power will deliver them from the wrath to come (1 Thess 1:10). In other words, their present affliction will be vindicated at the end, when Jesus will return in power.

Later in that same letter (1 Thess 4:13-18), Paul offers consolation to those Thessalonians whose fellow Christians have died before the coming of Jesus in power. Those Christians who have already died will not be at a disadvantage at the coming of Jesus on the clouds of heaven. He then exhorts them to live lives befitting the children of light which they are for "God has not destined us for wrath, but to obtain salvation through our Lord Jesus Christ (1 Thess 5:9).

These sections of 1 Thessalonians indicate Paul's dependence on a traditional early Christian apocalyptic outlook for his interpretation of suffering. The suffering that Christians are now experiencing will be vindicated by the coming of Jesus in power at the end of the age. The suffering of the present time takes on meaning only in the light of a future vindication.

This viewpoint will always be a part of Paul's understanding of human suffering. It is expressed most eloquently in 2 Corinthians 4:16-18; 5:6-10:

> [16]So we do not lose heart. Though our outer nature is wasting away, our inner nature is being renewed every day. [17]For this slight momentary affliction is preparing for us an eternal weight

of glory beyond all comparison, [18]because we look not to the things that are seen but to the things that are unseen; for the things that are seen are transient, but the things that are unseen are eternal . . . [6]So we are always of good courage; we know that while we are at home in the body we are away from the Lord, [7]for we walk by faith not by sight. [8]We are of good courage, and we would rather be away from the body and at home with the Lord. [9]So whether we are at home or away, we make it our aim to please him. [10]For we must all appear before the judgment seat of Christ, so that each one may receive good or evil, according to what he has done in the body.

Human suffering and affliction are seen in the light of a future judgment, at which time those Christians who have endured suffering in this present life will be rewarded at the time of the final judgment. Human suffering is seen in the light of Jesus' coming in power.

Put Paul also develops a somewhat different understanding of human suffering, an understanding which goes beyond the traditional apocalyptic viewpoint that present suffering will result in future reward. This new viewpoint takes different forms, but what is common to all of them is that they attempt to give meaning to human suffering not simply in the light of future vindication or reward but also as part of one's present existence.

One of the forms that this viewpoint takes is that human suffering and affliction are to be endured for the sake of the preaching of the Gospel. This viewpoint is found in 1 Corinthians 4:8-13 where Paul chides the Corinthian Christians for their claim to be already glorified. Paul points out sarcastically to them that, although they claim to be glorified, real preachers of the gospel (such as Paul himself) are continually called on to suffer for the sake of the gospel.

The most eloquent defense of this viewpoint, however, is to be found in 2 Corinthians 6:1-6. In this passage, again directed to the Corinthian Christians, Paul enumerates all of the affliction that he has endured for the sake of his ministry.

> ³We put no obstacle in any one's way, so that no fault may be found with our ministry, ⁴But as servants of God we commend ourselves in every way: through great endurance, in affliction, hardships, calamities, ⁵beatings, imprisonments, tumults, labors, watching, hunger; ⁶by purity, knowledge, forbearance, kindness, the Holy Spirit, genuine love, ⁷truthful speech, and the power of God.

In this viewpoint, human suffering and affliction take on meaning because they are endured for the sake of the preaching of the gospel. As Paul points out at the end of this passage, such endurance is made possible by the presence of the Holy Spirit and the power of God.

A second way in which Paul develops his understanding of human suffering beyond the traditional apocalyptic outlook is to assimilate it to the death of Jesus. Through suffering the Christian's life becomes more and more modeled on the suffering and death of Jesus. Perhaps the clearest example of this is found in 2 Corinthians 4:7-12:

> ⁷But we have this treasure in earthen vessels, to show that the transcendent power belongs to God and not to us. ⁸We are afflicted in every way, but not crushed; perplexed, but not driven to despair; ⁹persecuted, but not forsaken; struck down, but not destroyed; ¹⁰always carrying in the body the death of Jesus, so that the life of Jesus may also be manifested in our bodies. ¹¹For while we live we are always being given up to death for Jesus' sake, so that the life of Jesus may be manifested in our mortal flesh. ¹²So death is at work in us but life in you.

This passage contains the notion of suffering for Jesus' sake (2 Cor 4:11), a viewpoint that we have already looked at above. But its main thrust moves in a somewhat different direction. Just as new life for all paradoxically became possible through the death of Jesus, so too that same life of Jesus is now made manifest through the suffering of the Christian. Suffering, then, for the sake of Jesus becomes a way by which the life of Jesus is manifested in the Christian. In this passage Paul expands on his understanding of baptism which is most fully expressed in Roman 6:1-11. In that passage Paul describes the Christian's baptism as a dying with Christ so that the Christian will eventually rise with Christ. The suffering endured by the Christian is a concrete way in which that baptismal assimilation to the model of Christ is carried out.

The third way in which Paul moves beyond the apocalyptic model of present suffering and future vindication is to see the suffering endured by the Christian as part of a gradual transformation of the Christian, a transformation that will be completed only at the resurrection. Paul talks of this transformation as a result of the Christian's justification by faith.

> [1]Therefore, since we are justified by faith, we have peace with God through our Lord Jesus Christ. [2]Through him we have obtained access to this grace in which we stand, and we rejoice in our hope of sharing the glory of God. [3]More than that, we rejoice in our sufferings, knowing that suffering produces endurance, [4]and endurance produces character, and character produces hope, [5]and hope does not disappoint us, because God's love has been poured into our hearts through the Holy Spirit which has been given to us. (Rom 5:1-5)

Here again, the imagery has shifted somewhat. It is not precisely suffering for the sake of the gospel, or suffering as an assimilation to the death of Christ. Rather, it is a way through which the Christian is transformed in preparation for sharing in the glory of God. It is a view that through suffering the Christian can be changed for the better, that suffering produces endurance, endurance produces character, and character produces hope, a hope that does not disappoint. It is important to emphasize that Paul is not suggesting simply the moralistic notion that hardship builds character. Rather he is pointing out that through God's love which has been poured out into the hearts of Christians through the Holy Spirit the suffering that a Christian endures can be the occasion for God's tranforming power to be at work.

All three of these developments were meant to offer some explanation of the meaning of human suffering that went beyond the notion that present suffering, while meaningless in the present, will be rewarded in the future. They are attempts to offer some present meaning to suffering. It is crucial to emphasize that Paul's explanations were not meant to suggest that suffering and affliction were things that the Christian should actively seek out. Paul was quite aware that we do not have to seek out suffering. Suffering seeks us out. Given the fact that suffering is inevitable (a fact that we moderns find hard to accept), what meaning is to be given to it? Is suffering only a surd, or can it have a meaning which is part of the transforming love of God? Paul's reflections on suffering are meant to suggest that such a meaning is possible for the Christian.

None of these three interrelated developments was simply a matter of armchair reflections on the part of Paul. Rather, they were attempts on his part to give meaning to the sufferings that he had endured in his own life. They were not someone else's questions; they were also his own. They were attempts to make sense of the sufferings that he had endured as an apostle of Christ. They had roots in Paul's own life. Those autobiographical roots can be seen no more clearly than in 2 Corinthians 11:16—12:10. We looked at part of this passage (2 Cor 12:1-10) when we discussed Paul's experience of God. But the passage also throws light on how Paul's own understanding of suffering was influenced by his experience of God. Paul sets his own experience as an apostle over against that of rival apostles. He "boasts" first of all of the suffering and affliction that he has endured as an apostle (2 Cor 11:16-33). He then goes on to "boast" of his own visions and revelations (2 Cor 12:1-6). In the end, however, his primary "boast" is the "thorn given me in the flesh" (2 Cor 12:7). This "thorn," as I suggested earlier, was some sort of chronic illness.

> [7]And to keep me from being too elated by the abundance of revelations, a thorn was given me in the flesh, a messenger of Satan, to harass me, to keep me from being too elated. [8]Three times I besought the Lord about this, that it should leave me; [9]but he said to me, "My grace is sufficient for you, for my power is made perfect in weakness." I will all the more gladly boast of my weaknesses, that the power of Christ may rest upon me. [10]For the sake of Christ, then, I am content with weaknesses, insults, hardships, persecutions, and calamities; for when I am weak, then I am strong. (2 Cor 12:7-10)

Paul's paradoxical experience of God is that through God's power his own weaknesses have been transformed into strength, that his own sufferings have become manifestations of God's strength. Through his experience of God, his apparent strength has been shown to be in reality weakness, and his apparent weaknesses have been transformed by God's power into real strengths. One suspects that at the root of Paul's reflections on the meaning of suffering, especially as those reflections go beyond the traditional early Christian apocalyptic understanding of suffering, is his experience of a God who has transformed him not primarily through his own strength but through his weaknesses.

Conclusion

When one steps back, then, and reflects on the ways in which Paul has reflected on both human hopes and human sufferings, one is once again struck by the extent to which those reflections were rooted in the two central convictions of Paul's life: his experience of God and his preaching to the Gentiles. His experience of the call to preach to the Gentiles drove him beyond traditional early Christian apocalyptic eschatology. His transforming experience of God led him beyond the traditional early Christian explanations of the meaning of human suffering. Perhaps here more than anywhere else, one gets a sense of the extent to which Paul's own religious sensibilities and central religious convictions gave direction to his reflections on other important issues of Christian life.

8

PAUL AND THE PEOPLE
OF THE COVENANT

Throughout this book I have emphasized the central significance that Paul's experience of the risen Christ played in his
life. I have pointed out, among other things, how everything in
Paul's life paled in comparison with that experience and the
power that emerged from it. Among the things that paled in
the light of that experience was the observance of the Mosaic
Law. For Paul the observance of the Mosaic Law as such was
no longer an obligation for Christians. In fact, he was adamantly opposed to those Christians, whether Jewish or Gentile,
who sought to maintain the observance of the Mosaic Law as
an obligation parallel to belief in Christ. For Paul there could
be nothing parallel to belief in Christ.

This did not mean, however, that the Mosaic Law or its
observance was something inherently wrong. Paul always
thought of the Mosaic Law as a gift from God, but a gift that
was meant to be temporary, that is, until the coming of Christ.
The fact that it did not accomplish and could not accomplish
what occurred in the coming of Jesus Christ did not mean that

161

it was something that was faulty from the very start. Quite the contrary, the Law, by making human beings aware of what was sinful, prepared for the coming of Christ.

Paul's opposition to Christian observance of the Mosaic Law, then, was not because he thought that the Law was inherently flawed but because he thought that its time had passed, that it had been replaced by faith in Christ. The Law had its place in God's plan, but it was out of place in the faith of Christians. All of this is important to keep in mind because misinterpretations of Paul have had a prominent place in the sorry history of Christian anti-Jewish polemic and in the even sorrier history of Christian anti-Semitism.

Paul and His Fellow Jews

There is, however, another aspect of the question that must also be taken into consideration, and that is the relationship of Paul's thought not to the Mosaic Law as such but to the Jewish people. It is the question of how Paul saw the relationship of Christians not to the Mosaic Covenant, but to the people of that Covenant.

This is a crucial question if one is ever to have a full sense of Paul's own spirituality. To gain an adequate sense of that centrality, one has to keep two very important things always in mind. The first emerges from the viewpoint that Paul had on eschatology, the subject of the previous chapter. Paul's own convictions about the consummation of the world were characterized by a strong sense of universality and inclusiveness. In his description of Christians' hopes for the future, Paul saw everything being put under the power of Christ. At the end of the world, the power of Christ would be revealed in its fullness, and Christ, in turn, would submit everything to the Father. Nothing was to be excluded. Paul's eschatology, then, differed from that of the Johannine tradition which emphasized the permanent opposition of the "world" to God.

The second thing that must be kept in mind is Paul's own Jewishness. Paul always saw himself as a Jew and was never ashamed of that fact. Although he counted everything loss in comparison to his experience of Christ, he nevertheless was proud to claim that he was a Jew and that he had properly observed the Mosaic Law prior to his belief in Christ (see Phil 3:3-8; 2 Cor 12:22). Paul would never deny that the Jews were the ones to whom the oracles of God, that is, the Scriptures, had been entrusted (Rom 3:1-2).

Romans 9—11

It is this combination of Paul's own sense of being Jewish, of belonging to the Jewish people, and his conviction that at the consummation of the world all things would be taken up and subjected to Christ that created a deep anguish for him. Were the Jewish people, most of whom did not have faith in Christ, to be part of this final consummation, and if so how was that to come about? This anguish emerges most clearly in the opening verses of Romans 9—11:

> [1]I am speaking the truth in Christ, I am not lying; my conscience bears me witness in the Holy Spirit, [2]that I have great sorrow and unceasing anguish in my heart. [3]For I could wish that I myself were accursed and cut off from Christ for the sake of my brethren, my kinsmen by race. [4]They are Israelites, and to them

> belong the sonship, the glory, the covenants, the giving of the
> law, the worship, and the promises; [5]to them belong the patri-
> archs, and of their race, according to the flesh, is the Christ. God
> who is over all be blessed for ever. Amen. (Rom 9:1-5)

It is to this anguishing question that Paul now turns in
Romans 9—11. It is no accident that these three chapters
follow immediately on Paul's description of his hopes for the
ultimate consummation of all things in Christ. That ultimate
consummation, if it is to be truly universal and inclusive, must
include the Jewish people. But how can that be if the Jewish
people have rejected faith in Christ? Has God rejected his
people? This was probably the most difficult question with
which Paul ever had to struggle. If each of us has his or her
own doubts about faith, this was Paul's.

Romans 9—11, then, serve as the climax of the whole letter
to the Romans. All of Paul's reflections in Romans on the
central problems of his own preaching of the gospel culminate
in the central question of the fate of the Jewish people. Paul's
anguished reflections on the fate of his own people take the
form of interpretations of the Scriptures which attempt to
answer a series of rhetorical questions (Rom 9:14, 19, 30;
10:14, 18; 11:1, 7, 11). After Paul's very personal introduction
to the question (Rom 9:1-5), the rest of Romans 9—11 falls
into three major sections:

9:6-29　　　　　The Mystery of God's Purpose

9:30—10:21　　The Mystery of Jewish Unbelief

11:1-36　　　　The Salvation of Israel

Romans 9:6-29: *The Mystery of God's Purpose*

The first major section (Rom 9:6-29) consists of scriptural reflections on the mystery of God's choices and the question of whether God has been unjust in those choices. Paul begins by claiming that "not all who are descended from Israel belong to Israel, and not all are children of Abraham because they are his descendants" (Rom 9:6-7). In Romans 9:6-13 Paul points out that the "children of Abraham" are not all of Abraham's descendants but only those who are "children of the promise," that is, those who are descendants of Isaac but not those who are descendants of Ishmael. In addition, not all of Isaac's sons are counted as children of the promise, but only Jacob. Paul uses two quotations in Romans 9:12-13 to make his point, one from Genesis: "The elder (Esau) shall serve the younger (Jacob)" (Gen 25:23); and the other from the prophet Malachi: "Jacob I loved, but Esau I hated" (Mal 1:2-3).

He emphasizes the fact that the choice of Jacob and Esau took place before they had even been born, that is, before they had done anything either good or bad (Rom 9:11). This was to continue God's purpose of election, an election not due to deeds performed by either Esau or Jacob but rooted in God's act of calling. He begins, then, by highlighting the scriptural fact that God calls those whom he wills.

The question that such a choice raises is whether or not God is being unjust or arbitrary. It is to this question that Paul turns in Romans 9:14-18. He claims that God is not at all unjust in such a choice. Once again he offers proof from the Scriptures, this time from the story of Moses and Pharaoh. In Romans 9:15 he quotes God's words to Moses: "I will have mercy on whom I have mercy, and I will have compassion on whom I have compassion" (Exod 33:19). In Romans 9:17 he then quotes God's words that Moses is to speak to Pharaoh: "I have raised you up for the very purpose of showing my power in you, so that my name may be proclaimed in all the earth" (Exod 9:16). This show of God's power will in the course of the story have terrible consequences for Pharaoh and the Egyptian people. Paul's commentary on these two quotations is found in verses 16 and 18:

> [16]So it depends not upon man's will or exertion, but upon God's mercy. . . [18]So that he (God) has mercy upon whomever he wills, and he hardens the heart of whomever he wills.

God, then, is not being unjust in his choices because he has made clear from the very beginning that his choices are not made on the basis of human actions but depend on his own mysterious will.

Paul then raises another rhetorical question: You will say to me then, "Why does he still find fault? For who can resist his will?" (Rom 9:19). If human beings cannot resist God's will, how can God still hold them responsible and punish them? Paul's response to this rhetorical question is a series of other rhetorical questions. He uses the metaphor of the potter and his clay. Just as the potter can mold the clay into any shape he wishes and can make vessels for all kinds of purposes, whether exalted or menial, so too cannot God do what he wishes with those whom he molded? Who can complain if God formed some of his creatures for destruction in order to show his wrath while he formed others for mercy in order to show forth his glory?

Paul then applies this metaphor to the relationship between Jews and Gentiles. Once again he turns to Scripture for his argument. He first of all quotes the prophet Hosea 2:25; 2:1 to support his conviction about the inclusion of the Gentiles:

> Those who are not my people
> I will call "my people,"
> and her who was not beloved
> I will call "my beloved."
> And in the very place where it was
>   said to them, "You are not my people,"
>   they will be called "sons of the living God." (Rom 9:25-26)

He then turns to two quotations from Isaiah to support his position on the Jews. The first of these quotations (Isa 10:22-23) talks about only a remnant being saved:

> Though the number of the sons of Israel be as the sand of the sea, only a remnant of them will be saved; for the Lord will execute his sentence upon the earth with rigor and dispatch. (Rom 9:27-28)

The second quotation (Isa 1:9) in Romans 9:29 laments that had the Lord not given them children, they would have become like Sodom and Gomorrah, that is, they would have been totally destroyed.

As one reads this whole passage (Rom 9:19-29), one is struck by its highly rhetorical character, filled as it is with rhetorical questions. But one is also struck by the terrifying nature of what is described in it. While one can admit that Paul has shown that there is no injustice in God's showing mercy to those to whom he wishes to show mercy and wrath to those to whom he chooses to show wrath, nevertheless the vision of such a God is still terrifying. God may not be unjust in being arbitrary, but he is still being arbitrary and that in itself seems inappropriate to God. One even wonders whether

Paul himself was convinced of the case that he had just made, especially given Paul's emphasis on the universality of God's mercy in Romans 8.

Romans 9:30—11:1: *The Mystery of Jewish Unbelief*

Paul himself will return to that issue in Romans 11, where he too will go well beyond what is contained in Romans 9:19-29. But before he does that he will first reflect on the question of why the Jewish people as a whole have not come to have faith in Christ (Rom 9:30—10:21). He begins by reformulating the point of the quotations from Hosea and Isaiah. The result is an ironic situation in which the Gentiles, who had not pursued righteousness, have now attained it, while Israel, which had pursued the righteousness based on the Law, has not succeeded in it (Rom 9:30-31). The reason for this is that Israel did not pursue righteousness based on faith, but proceeded as if it were based on the Law.

In Romans 10:1-4 Paul once again expresses his own anguish at this situation. His heart's desire and his prayer is that Israel be saved. He goes on to emphasize their zeal, but he then points out that their zeal is without proper understanding. Because of ignorance, they sought their own righteousness rather than the righteousness of God. When Paul speaks of ignorance or lack of understanding in this context, he really means that they did not understand what is contained in the Scriptures. What they did not understand was that Christ is the goal and end of the Law, that in him everyone, Jew and Gentile alike, may be justified (Rom 10:4).

He then goes on to offer two further arguments, one to show that faith in Christ is not too difficult for them (Rom 10:5-13) and the other to show that they have already had the good news of the gospel preached to them (Rom 10:14-21).

The first of these arguments is rooted in an interpretation of Deuteronomy 30:11-14. In that passage Moses, speaking in the name of God, emphasizes to the Israelites that the commandment that has been given to them is not too difficult for them to observe.

> [11]For this commandment which I command you this day is not too hard for you, neither is it far off. [12]It is not in heaven, that you should say, "Who will go up for us to heaven, and bring it to us, that we may hear it and do it?" [13]Neither is it beyond the sea, that you should say, "Who will go over the sea for us, and bring it to us, that we may hear it and do it?" [14]But the word is very near you: it is in your mouth and in your heart, so that you can do it.

Paul applies this text to the preaching of the Christian message. This "word" does not require someone to go up to heaven, as if to bring Christ down, or to go down to the underworld, as if to bring Christ up. Rather, like the word in Deuteronomy 30:14, this word is near, in one's heart and on one's lips (Rom 10:8). This word involves two central elements, first faith in the Lord Jesus whom God raised from the dead, and second that *everyone* who calls upon the name of the Lord will be saved (Rom 10:9, 13). These two elements reflect once again Paul's two central convictions: first, the centrality of Christ and of faith in him; and second, the belief that there is no longer a distinction between Jew and Gentile, so that both Jew and Gentile can now be saved (Rom 10:12). Neither of those two elements is too difficult to believe.

Paul's second argument (Rom 10:14-21) deals, once again in very rhetorical fashion, with the question of whether or not Israel has had a chance to hear that word. At least rhetorically this argument is meant to deal with the objection that, granted the word is not too difficult to believe, still the question is whether Israel has had a chance to hear that word. Paul's argument is that they have heard the word. To substantiate this he quotes Psalms 19:5, which he takes to refer to the preaching of the Gospel:

> Their voice has gone out to all the earth,
> and their words to the ends of the world.

They have, then, had the opportunity to hear that word, but they have not accepted it.

Paul concludes this section with three further quotations from the Scriptures, one from Deuteronomy (Deut 32:21) and two from Isaiah (Isa 65:1, 2). These quotations all emphasize that the good news of the Gospel has gone out to the Gentiles who have accepted it, but that it has been rejected by Israel even though it has been continually offered to them.

All of these quotations from the Scriptures were meant to substantiate Paul's main point, presented at the beginning of Romans 10, that Israel has been zealous for God but that its zeal has been without understanding because it did not understand the Scriptures. Yet there is no excuse for their lack of understanding, especially since the Scriptures point out that the word is not too difficult to believe and that it has been preached to them. Once again the rhetoric of this section leads one to feel that the situation is really hopeless, that there is nothing more to be done.

Romans 11:1-36: The Salvation of All Israel

One is not surprised, then, at Paul's rhetorical question in Romans 11:1 that begins the last section of his anguished reflections on the fate of Israel (Rom 11:1-36): I ask, then, has God rejected his people? But one is surprised by the answer that he so quickly gives to the question: By no means! After the arguments of the preceding two chapters which seem to lead to the conclusion that God has rejected Israel for its unbelief, Paul makes an about-face and begins to explain the real thrust of all of these arguments: God has not rejected his people whom he foreknew (Rom 11:2). Paul goes about making his final argument in four steps:

11:1-10	The Remnant of Israel
11:11-24	The Salvation of the Gentiles
11:25-32	The Restoration of Israel
11:33-36	Final Hymn of Praise to God

In the first section (Rom 11:1-10), Paul develops the image of the "remnant of Israel." He uses the example of the accusation of the prophet Elijah against Israel. In 1 Kings 19:10, 14 the prophet Elijah complains to God that Israel has killed the prophets and destroyed the altars used to offer sacrifices to God. Elijah claims that he alone has remained faithful to God. But God's reply to Elijah is that Elijah as a matter of fact is not alone. God has kept a "remnant of Israel," seven thousand who have not turned to worship Baal, the Canaanite god (1 Kgs 19:18). There were more who remained faithful than Elijah was willing to admit.

Paul argues that the same is true of the present day, that a faithful remnant chosen by grace remains. That remnant is made up of people like Paul, who are Israelites and descendants of Abraham and who have, by grace, come to have faith. The elect have obtained grace, but the others were hardened. That hardening, however, was part of God's plan; it is God who gave them a spirit of stupor (Rom 11:8/Deut 29:3) and God who let their eyes be darkened (Rom 11:10/Ps 69:23).

Paul's first step, then, was to begin by emphasizing that, in fact, a remnant of faithful Israelites still did exist. His second step (Rom 11:11-24) is to go even further, to claim that Israel's failure was part of a larger plan to bring salvation to the Gentiles.

> [11]So I ask, have they stumbled so as to fall? By no means! But through their trespass salvation has come to the Gentiles, so as to make Israel jealous. [12]Now if their trespass means riches for the world, and if their failure means riches for the Gentiles, how much more will their full inclusion mean? (Rom 11:11-12)

Israel's failure was not meant to result in Israel's rejection by God. Rather, Israel's failure was meant to lead to salvation for the Gentiles. If that is the case, then, how much more significant will Israel's final inclusion in salvation be? Once again Paul brings in one of his central convictions, the salvation of the Gentiles through grace and faith. But here he carries that conviction one step further. If salvation came to the Gentiles, at least partially because of Israel's apparent rejection of grace, then surely Israel cannot have been really rejected by God. Their apparent "rejection," rather, was part of a larger plan of salvation that would ultimately also include them.

At this point in the letter, Paul specifically addresses those among his readers who are Gentiles (Rom 11:13-24). He emphasizes to them that his own ministry to the Gentiles was not simply to convert the Gentiles but also to make his fellow Jews "jealous" and so bring them to salvation (Rom 11:14). He even claims that, if the rejection of Israel meant the reconciliation of the world, that is, the salvation of the Gentiles, then the acceptance of Israel can mean nothing less than the resurrection of the dead, that is, the final consummation of the world (Rom 11:15).

He also warns Gentile Christians against boasting about their inclusion and Israel's rejection. He uses an example taken from the cultivation of olive trees. The Gentiles are branches from wild olive trees that have been grafted onto cultivated olive trees. They were grafted onto olive trees some of whose natural branches (that is, Israel) have been cut off. But this is nothing to boast of. If they were grafted onto the cultivated olive tree through God's kindness, they can just as easily be cut off again if they prove themselves unworthy. Conversely, if Israel does not persist in its unbelief, it can just as easily be grafted onto the olive tree again. As a matter of fact, they will most certainly be grafted on again.

> [24]For if you (the Gentiles) have been cut from what is by nature a wild olive tree, and grafted, contrary to nature, into a cultivated olive tree, how much more will these natural branches be grafted back onto their own olive tree. (Rom 11:24)

Paul emphasizes his conviction that salvation for the Gentiles cannot mean the ultimate rejection of the Jews. Israel's failure was for the sake of the Gentiles and their salvation; but, then, the salvation of the Gentiles must ultimately result in a like salvation for the Jews.

These reflections bring Paul to the climax of his anguished thoughts about his fellow Jews (Rom 11:25-32), the restoration of *all* Israel. In these verses he sums up his thoughts about the relationship of Jew and Gentile in the mysterious plan of God for the salvation of all:

> [25]Lest you be wise in your own conceits, I want you to understand this mystery, brethren: a hardening has come upon part of Israel, until the full number of the Gentiles come in, [26]and so all Israel will be saved; as it is written,
> "The Deliverer will come from Zion,
> he will banish all ungodliness from Jacob";
> [27]"and this will be my covenant with them
> when I take away their sins." (Isa 59:20-21; 27:9; Jer 31:33).
> [28]As regards the gospel they (the Jews) are enemies of God, for your sake; but as regards election they are beloved for the sake of their forefathers. [29]For the gifts and call of God are irrevocable. [30]Just as you were once disobedient to God but now have received mercy because of their disobedience, [31]so they now have been disobedient in order that by the mercy shown to you they also may receive mercy. [32]For God has consigned all men to disobedience, that he may have mercy upon all. (Rom 11:25-32)

In this passage Paul takes up and develops in a new direction the language that he has been using in the rest of the letter. For the first time in the letter he now talks about the salvation of *all* Israel and contrasts that salvation with the hardening that had come upon *part* of Israel (Rom 11:25-26). In Romans 9:27-28 and Romans 11:5 Paul pointed to a remnant of Israel which would be saved or chosen by grace. Now he expresses his conviction that in the mysterious plan of God *all* Israel will be saved. In the end, the salvation of only a remnant of Israel is not enough. While at the present time only a remnant of Israel has proved faithful, in the end all Israel will find salvation.

Second, Paul takes up the language that he has used earlier in this section of the letter about the hardening of Israel as the opportunity for the inclusion of the Gentiles (Rom 11:13-16). Only now he turns it around. Just as the Gentiles were once disobedient but now have received mercy, so too Israel through whose disobedience mercy was shown to the Gentiles will also find mercy (Rom 11:30-31). Paul's conviction that the disobedient Gentiles have found mercy is now developed into the conviction that disobedient Israel will also find mercy.

Third, Paul sums up his position about the ultimate salvation of Israel by claiming that "God has consigned all men to disobedience, that he may have mercy on all" (Rom 11:32). Here he takes up the viewpoint that he expressed at the beginning of Romans that "since all have sinned and fall short of the glory of God, they are justified by his grace as a gift, through the redemption which is in Christ Jesus" (Rom 3:23-24). In the passage from Romans 3, Paul was claiming that since all have sinned, Jew and Gentile alike, all stand equally in need of God's mercy. His point was to show the equality of Jew and Gentile in sinfulness. In Romans 11:32 he expresses the positive side of that earlier conviction. If Jew and Gentile are equally sinful and equally in need of God's mercy, then both will equally obtain that mercy. Since the gift and call of God to the Jews is irrevocable (Rom 11:29), God will show them at least as much mercy as he has shown to Gentiles. If the Gentiles are to be saved, then so too are the Jews, and not simply a small remnant.

What began then in Romans 9:1-5 as anguished questions about the ultimate future of his own people ends with a hymn of praise to the marvelous yet inscrutable wisdom of God:

> ³³O the depth of the riches and wisdom and knowledge of God!
> How unsearchable are his judgments and how inscrutable his
> ways!
> > ³⁴"For who has known the mind of the Lord,
> > or who has been his counselor?"
> > ³⁵"Or who has given a gift to him
> > that he might be repaid?"
> ³⁶For from him and through him and to him are all things. To
> him be glory for ever. Amen. (Rom 11:33-36)

Once again, Paul's conviction of the universality of God's mercy and plan of salvation comes to the surface. Because Paul could not imagine that God's mercy was anything less than universal, he could not imagine that the Jews would be excluded from God's ultimate gift of salvation. Romans 9—11, then, serve as a climax of the letter in that the central problem raised by the universality and inclusiveness expressed in Romans 8, that is, the problem of Jewish unbelief, finds its answer in Romans 11 in the depths of the wisdom and knowledge of God.

It is interesting to note in Romans 11 that Paul does not mention the figure of Christ when he talks of the ultimate salvation of Israel. This has led some interpreters to suggest that the figure of Christ does not play a role in the ultimate salvation of the Jews in Paul's mind. Rather, just as the Gentiles are ultimately saved through Christ, the Jews are ultimately saved through the promises made in the Torah. In this interpretation the Torah remains the means of salvation for the Jews, just as Christ has now become the means of salvation for the Gentiles.

This interpretation, however, does not take into considera-

tion the context within which Romans 9—11 occurs. Romans
9—11 is meant to deal with the problem created by the
universality and inclusiveness of salvation *in Christ* developed
in Romans 8. Paul expresses this same universality and inclusiveness in 1 Corinthians 15:20-28. In that section "all things
are put in subjection to him," that is, in subjection to Christ.
Both Romans 8 and 1 Corinthians 15 assume that Christ is
central to the salvation of both Jew and Gentile, as a matter of
fact, central to the salvation of all of creation. Romans 11 must
be interpreted in that context, and in such a context Christ
must also play a central role in Paul's mind in the ultimate
salvation of the Jews.

It is, nevertheless, interesting that Paul does not explicitly
mention Christ in Romans 11. While one must assume a
central role for Christ in the ultimate salvation of the Jews
based on Romans 8, Paul is vague about just how that central
role will ultimately play itself out. Similar to his unwillingness
in 1 Corinthians 15:35-50 to describe in any detail the reality
of the resurrected body, Paul is certain of the ultimate salvation of his fellow Jews and yet is equally certain that how
exactly that will occur is a tremendous mystery. Both at the
end of 1 Corinthians 15 (1 Cor 15:51) and Romans 11 (Rom
11:25) Paul emphasizes the mysterious character of God's
merciful providence. He is convinced of *that*, but he does not
know the *how*.

Conclusion

If it is true that any authentic faith must be willing to face
honestly those doubts that are part of any human being's life,

then these anguished chapters in Romans represent Paul's attempt to face those doubts. On the one hand, one sees Paul's deep disappointment that his fellow Jews have not come to have faith in Christ. On the other hand, his deep attachment to his fellow Jews and his conviction that God's irrevocable promises to Israel will not be in vain led him to believe, against his own personal experience, that those promises would bear fruit and ultimately prove true.

Paul's attachment to his fellow Jews and to God's promises to them point to the utter incompatibility of Paul's Christian faith with any kind of anti-Semitism. While Paul's own hopes for his fellow Jews are very different from the hopes that his fellow Jews had and have for themselves, those differences do not lead Paul to claim that Israel has been rejected by God or that the promises made by God to Israel have been in vain. The anti-Semitic uses to which Paul has been put over the centuries are utterly at variance with Paul's own hopes and his deepest convictions about the universality of God's merciful love. While Christians and Jews differ over some of the central elements of their respective faiths, they both share the central conviction about that love. This conviction cannot serve as a basis for anti-Semitism; after all, Paul derived it from his interpretation of the promises made to Abraham, the father of both faiths.

CONCLUSION

THE IMAGE OF THE BODY

As one looks at the spirituality of Paul, one can see in it elements which are familiar, such as the centrality of faith in Christ, the power of the Spirit, the necessity of love. These elements have always played a central role in the life of the Church; they have been ideals even when individual Christians and the Church as a whole have not lived up to them. Yet we have to remind ourselves that the spirituality of Paul which we have looked at in the course of this book was not something "familiar" to Paul and other early Christians. For them the articulation and working out of these realities was something new. From the traditions and beliefs of Judaism, Paul and other early Christians had important guides but no detailed road maps. What seems familiar to us has become familiar only because of the power and influence of early Christians like Paul.

Without benefit of clear guidelines and precedents, Paul tried to hold in a creative tension beliefs and values that did not automatically or effortlessly go together. He tried to be true to both his Jewish heritage and his experience of Christ. He was firmly convinced that Jesus was the Messiah awaited by the Jews and yet that his experience of that same Jesus called him to preach to the Gentiles a Gospel without the

179

observance of the Mosaic Law. He sought to reconcile the reality of Christian freedom with Christian responsibility for the well-being of the community. Finally, he sought to reconcile his convictions about the future consummation of the world in Christ with the realities of both present human suffering and the fact that most of his fellow Jews did not accept his own beliefs about Christ.

He tried to work all of this out as part of a life spent traveling around the eastern half of the Mediterranean basin, a life spent founding and guiding various Christian communities. He was successful in some of these efforts. One of those successes was probably his guidance of the independent and sometimes unruly community at Corinth. Yet, we are less certain of the success of some of his other efforts. We do not know, for example , whether he was successful in convincing the Galatian Christians not to combine their belief in Christ with the observance of the Mosaic Law. Nor are we sure that his attempts to stay on good terms with the Jewish Christian community in Jerusalem were successful. He was, perhaps, less successful than we are tempted to believe.

We are also tempted to ask whether he would have been more successful had he taken another tack, had he been less forthright or blunt with the Galatian Christians, had he been more willing to compromise with the misgivings that Jewish Christians had about his preaching to the Gentiles without the observance of the Mosaic Law. Hindsight, however, has a deceptive clarity to it. Paul, like the rest of us, was very human, both in his virtues and in his shortcomings; and a good part of our fascination with him is that very combination of virtues and vices. He could have done things a bit differently, but then he would not have been the same Paul.

When one looks for a way to sum up Paul's convictions and concerns, one could do worse than to point to the image of the body of Christ. Paul has a number of ways of talking about the unity of Christ and Christians in his letters: the experience of the Spirit (Gal 3:1-5); assimilation to the death and resurrection of Christ (Rom 6:1-11); Christians as temples of the Holy Spirit (1 Cor 6:15-20). One of the most prominent images, however, is that of the Church as the Body of Christ.

The image of the Church as the Body of Christ does not as such appear in Paul's earlier letters. It comes to prominence only in 1 Corinthians and Romans. The image became a way for Paul to bring into focus his concerns for both the unity of Christians in Christ and the unity and diversity among Christians themselves.

The image of the one body with many members appears most prominently in 1 Corinthians 12:12-31. It appears in the context of Paul's discussion of the variety of "spiritual gifts" (see 1 Cor 12:1-11). As I mentioned before, Paul, in writing to the Christian community at Corinth, was trying among other things to overcome the numerous factions and divisions in the community. Among the causes of these divisions were the claims of various Corinthian Christians to different "spiritual gifts," for example prophecy, miracle working, speaking in tongues, "knowledge", etc. (1 Cor 12:4-11). These claims divided rather than unified them.

Paul begins by emphasizing that while there are varieties of gifts, there is but one Spirit; while there are varieties of service, there is but one Lord; and while there are varieties of working, there is but one God who inspires them all (1 Cor 12:4-6). Paul's point is to emphasize that the diversity of gifts must be seen within the larger context of the unity of the Christian community in God.

He then changes the image that he uses and in 1 Corinthians 12:12-31 develops the image of the Christian community as the body of Christ. This section of the letter is divided into three parts:

1 Cor 12:12-13:   The Church as the body of Christ

1 Cor 12:14-26:   The body as a "political" metaphor

1 Cor 12:27-31:   The Church once again as the body of Christ combined with the body as a "political" metaphor

The middle part of this section (1 Cor 12:14-26) develops a metaphor that was common in the ancient world. It is the metaphor of a civil community as a "body politic." Just as the human body is composed of many parts but all of the parts work together for the good of the whole, so too civil society is composed of many members but all of the members should work for the good of the whole, the common good. Paul applies this metaphor to the Christian community. Although the Christian community is composed of many members who have been given a variety of gifts, all of the members of the community should use those gifts for the good of the whole community.

Yet, Paul means to use the image of the body as more than a metaphor. In more than a metaphorical sense, the Christian community is the body of Christ. This emerges at the beginning (1 Cor 12:12-13) and at the end (1 Cor 12:27-31) of this section. In 1 Corinthians 12:12-13 Paul is speaking more than metaphorically:

> [12]For just as the body is one and has many members, and all the members of the body, though many, are one body, so it is with

> Christ. [13]For by one Spirit we were all baptized into one body—Jews or Greeks, slaves or free—and all were made to drink of one Spirit.

In this passage Paul is not comparing the human body with its many members to the Christian community with its many members. That would still be the metaphorical use of the body image. Rather, he compares the human body and its many members with Christ and his many members. Through baptism, Christians, whether Jews or Greeks, slaves or free, are baptized into one body, the body of Christ.

In addition, "all were made to drink of one Spirit." That may very well be a reference to the Christian eucharist. That suspicion is further strengthened by a passage from earlier in 1 Corinthians:

> [16]The cup of blessing which we bless, is it not a participation in the blood of Christ? The bread that we break, is it not a participation in the body of Christ? [17]Because there is one bread, we who are many are one body, for we all partake of the one bread. (1 Cor 10:16-17)

By participation in the cup and the bread of the eucharist, that is, in the body and blood of Christ, Christians, although many, become one body, that is, the body of Christ. Through baptism and participation in the eucharist, Christians become members of the body of Christ, a body which is much more than a metaphorical way of talking about group solidarity.

At the end of this section (1 Cor 12:27-31) Paul combines the notion of the Christian community as the body of Christ through baptism and the eucharist with the body as a political metaphor.

> [27]Now you are the body of Christ and individually members of
> it. [28]And God has appointed in the church first apostles, second
> prophets, third teachers, then workers of miracles, then healers,
> helpers, administrators, speakers in various kinds of tongues.
> [29]Are all apostles? Are all prophets? Are all teachers? Do all
> work miracles? [30]Do all possess gifts of healing? Do all speak
> with tongues? Do all interpret? [31]But earnestly desire the
> higher gifts.

Paul has taken his conviction of the Christian community as
the body of Christ and combined it with the political metaphor of the body politic and then applied it specifically to
emphasize the diversity in unity in the Christian community.
Because the Christian community is the body of Christ, all of
its various members with their various gifts and responsibilities must all work for the good of the whole, the common good
of the body of Christ.

As he has done so often before, Paul has taken ideas and
metaphors that were traditional and combined them in such a
way as to move his thought in a new direction. The use of the
metaphor of the body for the description of a social unit was
widespread in the ancient world. Likewise, the idea that
baptism and the eucharist made Christians members of the
body of Christ may well have been an idea that was already
part of Christian tradition. What was original with Paul was
the combination of the two elements and the development of
thought that resulted from that combination. Paul once again
has tried to hold together the polarities of tradition and
originality.

This combination, however, has enabled Paul to accomplish three other things, all of which are characteristic of Paul's
central convictions and concerns. First, it offers him another

way of speaking about the unity between Christ and Christians. Through baptism and the eucharist Christians become members of the body of Christ. The importance of talking about the unity of Christ and Christians as a bodily unity is that it offers Paul a way of describing that unity in corporate or communitarian terms. The relationship is not simply between Christ and the individual Christian but between Christ and Christians as a community.

Second, it offers Paul a way to emphasize the responsibilities that Christians have for one another. After claiming in 1 Corinthians 10:16-17 that participation in the one bread of the eucharist makes Christians members of the one body of Christ, he can go on in 1 Corinthians 11:17-34 to chide the Corinthian Christians for their conduct at the eucharist. The wealthy bring expensive food while the poor go hungry at the eucharistic celebrations. This is an offense against the unity of the community. But it also is to profane the body and blood of the Lord (1 Cor 11:27). The body of Christ, then, is inextricably bound up with the unity of the Christian community.

Finally, in speaking of the body of Christ Paul is able to talk about the unity and diversity of the Christian community. He is able to hold together the polarities of legitimate Christian freedom and of sensitivity to the needs of the Christian community as a whole. In 1 Corinthians 12 Paul can claim that there are a variety of gifts in the community; yet all of these gifts must be seen in the light of their contribution to the good of the Christian community as a whole.

The image of the body of Christ, then, is an apt way to end our look at the spirituality of St. Paul. Paul's spirituality is one that is developed and lived out in the midst of everyday life. It is not systematic but is formed on the basis of several central convictions, convictions rooted in his own experience and in that of the Christian communities of which he was a part. Those convictions about the power of God, the centrality of Christ, and the universality of salvation were worked out in the mire and muddle of living.

In living out those central convictions, Paul tried to hold together his own experience and that of other Christians and Christian tradition; he tried to combine a hope for the future consummation of the world in Christ with a clearheaded vision of the reality of human suffering, sin, and death; he tried to reconcile Christian freedom with Christian love and responsibility for others. His solutions to those tensions may not in all cases be ours; but in all cases they do challenge us; and in any case our own living out of the Christian faith must deal with those same tensions and be true to those same hopes.

FOR FURTHER READING

Rudolf Bultmann. *The Theology of the New Testament.* 2 vols. New York: Scribner's, 1951-55. 1.185-352.

James D. G. Dunn. *Christology in the Making: A New Testament Inquiry into the Origins of the Doctrine of the Incarnation.* Philadelphia: Westminster, 1980.

Joseph A. Fitzmyer. *Pauline Theology, A Brief Sketch.* Englewood-Cliffs, N.J.: Prentice-Hall, 1967.

Leander Keck. *Paul and His Letters.* Philadelphia: Fortress, 1979.

Wayne A. Meeks. *The First Urban Christians: The Social World of the Apostle Paul.* New Haven: Yale University, 1983.

Jerome Murphy-O'Connor. *Becoming Human Together: The Pastoral Anthropology of St. Paul.* Good News Studies 2. Wilmington, Del.: Michael Glazier, 1982.

E. P. Sanders. *Paul, the Law, and the Jewish People.* Philadelphia: Fortress, 1983.

Krister Stendahl. *Paul Among Jews and Gentiles.* Philadelphia: Fortress, 1976.

Gerd Theissen. *The Social Setting of Pauline Christianity: Essays on Corinth.* Philadelphia: Fortress, 1982.

SUBJECT INDEX

BIBLICAL INDEX